HISTORIC SAMPLERS

HISTORIC SAMPLERS

SELECTED FROM MUSEUMS AND HISTORIC HOMES
With 30 cross-stitch charts for authentic reproduction

Patricia Ryan and
Allen D. Bragdon

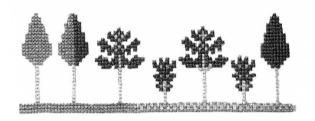

A BULFINCH PRESS BOOK
Little, Brown and Company
Boston • Toronto • London

This book is dedicated to the children who stitched the samplers

Patricia Ryan, who arranged with the museums and historical associations for the publication of the samplers in this collection, charted them, stitched most of the replicas, and collected the information from which this book was written, expresses her thanks to her parents, Francis and Dorothy Ryan, for their total support and love during the three-year process of preparing the material for this book, and to Betsy Bergen Hinkley for her friendship, support, and sharing her family. Patricia also gratefully expresses her thanks to other members of her family, extended family, and friends who opened their homes to her in her travels, including Dr. Richard M. and Ethel Ryan, Christopher and Stephanie Beard O'Neill and their daughters Catlin and Abby, Daniel and Nancy Bergen, Ernest and Terry Bergen Lewis, as well as to Pat Rufo for her faith and a phone call.

We wish to express our thanks to the directors, curators and staff members of all the institutions in whose care these samplers have been for permission to chart them and for supplying us with the necessary provenance. Especially helpful to Patricia were the late Silvio Conti and his office staff, who directed her to Agnes Mullin at Arlington House, and Colleen Callahan of the Valentine Museum.

The following people deserve special mention for the generous contribution of their knowledge and for their professional skills.

Zweigart supplied the fine linens in a variety of thread counts used to replicate the antique samplers.

For help in charting parts of samplers: Cynthia Sweeney Chilauskas, Carol Siwa, Daniel Bergen, Catlin O'Neill, Nancy Porteus, and Cynthia Doane.

ACKNOWLEDGMENTS

For help in stitching some of the replicas shown in the photographs: Karen Fitzgerald Zimmerman, Carol and Emily Louise Siwa, Cynthia Sweeney Chilauskas, and the ladies of the Cross Stitch shop.

For framing the finished samplers, Jimmy Junsan.

Allen Bragdon, who conceived the idea for this book and who collaborated in the writing of it, expresses his appreciation for the contributions of those artists and freelance professionals who helped design, edit, illustrate, photograph, and lay out the pages, namely: John Miller, designer; Arnold Eliason, mechanical production manager; Jill Farinelli, and Donald W. Davidson, editors; Ed Kadunk, illustrator; Ned Manter and Patrick Weisman, photographers; Jim Canavan, Carolyn Zellers, Walter Noel, Lianne Dunn, and Sean Walsh, who helped organize graphics and did electronic page formatting.

Picture Credits: Page 9 — Courtesy of the Print Collection, Miriam & Ira D. Wallach Division of Art, Prints and Photographs, The New York Public Library, Astor, Lenox and Tilden Foundations. Page 10 — Courtesy of the Free Library of Philadelphia. Page 11 — Courtesy of the Pilgrim Society, Plymouth, Massachusetts; photograph by Alan Harvey. Page 13 — Courtesy of Indiana University, Bloomington, Indiana, Lilly Library. We wish to acknowledge reference to primary source research by Davida Tenenbaum Deutsch for an article in *Antiques*.

The cross stitch motifs on the cover were copied from an antique sampler stitched c. 1800 by Sarah Pelham, age six.

Text copyright © 1992 by Patricia Ryan
Illustrations and compilation copyright © 1992 by Allen D. Bragdon Publishers, Inc.

Designed by Allen D. Bragdon Publishers, Inc.

First Edition
ISBN 0-8212-1931-6

Library of Congress Catalog Card Number 91-58930
Library of Congress Cataloging-in-Publication information is available.

Bulfinch Press is an imprint and trademark of Little, Brown and Company (Inc.)
Published simultaneously in Canada by Little, Brown & Company (Canada) Limited

PRINTED IN HONG KONG

LOCATIONS OF THE ORIGINAL SAMPLERS

The samplers in this collection were selected and charted in cooperation with the following institutions. Local historical societies often have samplers as interesting as those in large institutions. Though many original samplers are not on public display, in most cases, they may be seen by calling ahead to make a specific appointment to view them.

Museum of Fine Arts, Boston
465 Huntington Avenue
Boston, Massachusetts 02115
(617) 267-9300
pages 24, 36, 68, 72, 132

The Essex Institute
132 Essex Street
Salem, Massachusetts 01970
(508) 744-3390
pages 28, 32, 54

Sandwich Glass Museum
Historical Society
129 Main Street, P.O. Box 103
Sandwich, Massachusetts 02563
(508) 888-0251
pages 102, 116

Daughters of the American
Revolution
Constitution Hall
Washington, D.C. 20016
(202) 628-4780
page 86

The Valentine Museum
1015 East Clay Street
Richmond, Virginia 23219
(804) 649-0711
pages 108, 138

Old York Historical Society
Box 312
York, Maine 03909
(207) 363-4974
page 142

Moravian Museum
1741 Gemein Haus
66 West Church Street
Bethlehem, Pennsylvania 18018
(215) 867-0173
page 122

Paul Revere House
Paul Revere Memorial
Association
10 North Square
Boston, Massachusetts 02113
(617) 523-2338
page 76

Dukes County Historical
Society
Martha's Vineyard
School and Cooke Streets
Edgartown, Massachusetts 02539
(508) 627-4441
page 20, 40

Bennington Museum
West Main Street
Bennington, Vermont 05201
(802) 447-1571
pages 16, 50, 126

Kenmore Association
1201 Washington Avenue
Fredericksburg, Virginia 22401
(703) 373-3381
page 64

Smithsonian Institution
Museum of American History
Washington, D.C. 20016
(202) 357-1889
page 150

Sandy Springs Museum
Tall Timbers
2707 Olney-Sandy Springs Rd.
Olney, Maryland 20860
(301) 774-0022
page 96

Arlington House, R. E. Lee
Memorial
Arlington National Cemetery
Arlington, Virginia 22210
pages 44, 58, 82

Margaret Woodbury Strong
Museum
1 Manhattan Square
Rochester, New York 14607
(703) 263-2700
page 112

Quakertown Historical Society
26 North Main Street, Box 846
Quakertown, Pennsylvania 18951
page 90

Montgomery County Historical
Society
Dawson House
103 West Montgomery Avenue
Rockville, Maryland 20850
(301) 762-149
page 146

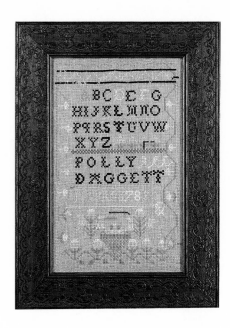

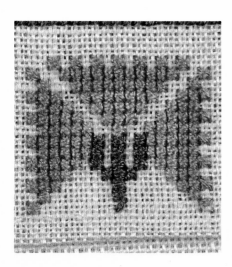

CONTENTS

This book is designed to permit people who enjoy doing decorative embroidery to accurately reproduce priceless antique samplers. The charts and colors have been approved by the curators of the museums and historical institutions who own the originals. They have insisted that the reproduction must match the original *exactly* as it appears today in their collection. There are two exceptions that have been slightly reconstructed under the guidance of their curators. One is the historically important sampler by Betty Washington Lewis from the Kenmore Association in Fredericksburg, Virginia. The color of the threads had faded so badly that significant portions were nearly illegible. In the other, by Eliza Hall at the Museum of Fine Arts, Boston, the threads in her over-one alphabet had disintegrated so much that the letters disappeared. Fortunately, the faint imprint the letters had left on the linen made it possible for us to reconstruct her stitches exactly.

The charts for all the samplers in this book replicate even the disintegrated threads, stitches left uncrossed or misplaced, hanging threads, and mends in the linen, as well as the exact colors of the original linen and threads. Hence the reconstructed replicas shown here in color are almost indistinguishable from the irreplaceable antiques in the museums. A listing of the museums holding the originals, with addresses and phone numbers, appears on an earlier page.

There are thirty samplers here, arranged roughly in chronological order starting with 1734 and ending in the late 1860s. We selected these specific samplers because they are among the most interesting examples of this venerable folk art extant in North America today. Some pre-date our nation. Some were stitched by relations of famous presidents, statesmen and patriots—one was even *stitched* by a legendary patriot of the Revolutionary War. Two are very rare examples of samplers by boys. Some are small, some huge; some are ornately decorative, some are modest marking samplers. Some will challenge even experienced needleworkers with excellent eyesight. Others, like the ones early in the book, are easy enough for a beginner to learn from. After all, by definition, samplers were only the first or second attempts at stitchery by children barely into their teens, and younger.

What is known about the child who stitched each sampler, and often that is very little, appears in a brief introduction to each sampler that faces the color photograph of the finished work. The pages following the photograph provide instructions and

HOW TO WORK THIS BOOK

charts for recreating the original as pictured. The instruction pages often include color enlargements of technically or decoratively interesting details from that sampler. We have followed contemporary conventions for presenting charts, legends, color-references and stitch abbreviations. As is traditional, one square on the chart equals two linen threads, hence one stitch is over two threads unless the chart symbol or instructions specify that the stitch is to be made over one thread, and over-ones appear very often. The precise positionings of over-one stitches are represented in the Chart Key by the location of solid fills in the box, as ◣, or by tiny crosses, as ✗. Convention stops there. The original stitchers did not follow tidy rules, such as burying waste knots or crossing each stitch the same direction, so our instructions must be similarly unconventional.

In order to reproduce complete charts some have been divided into sections which appear on facing or following pages. In every case at least five rows of the grid overlap from section to section. The strips that overlap carry a light grey tint. We heartily encourage you to copy the charts for your private use so you need not carry the book in your work bag. Most photocopy machines now allow you to enlarge as you copy.

On the instruction page the dimensions of the stitched area appear in italics beneath the child's name. The recommended dimensions of the linen to buy, along with the thread-count and color are given in the "Materials" paragraph. If the thread-count is too fine to see conveniently, from the given specifications you will easily be able to calculate the design size of the sampler stitched on a looser weave. Since standard colors of commercially available linen do not match the antiques exactly, instructions for dying the fabric appear with the materials and in the General Instructions in the Appendix.

Almost all the originals were stitched with silk thread which retains its sheen. Since the color palette of commercially-available silk embroidery thread is too limited to match the original samplers, the Chart Keys specify DMC floss because sheen and an exact color match were considered more important than the material by the curators of the original works. Following current convention, unless otherwise noted in the Chart Key use two strands of floss, (which is equivalent in thickness to one strand of most of the original silk threads used in these samplers). Where thicker or thinner threads were used, the key or instructions specifies the correct number of strands.
— PR and ADB

INTRODUCTION

This book details the work in thirty remarkable samplers that have endured from this nation's earliest years. Passed down as family heirlooms through several generations, these extraordinary examples of handworked embroidery now remain in the care of museums and historical societies, as well as historic homes. None of these rare and valuable pieces was ever intended to serve as mere decoration. They were stitched as a proof of a practical skill and a record of how to form initials for marking linens. Now they have become works of art and primary-source, historical artifacts that, under close examination, yield up vivid and often poignant insights into the surroundings and personalities of the children who stitched them.

With the exception of two very rare examples wrought by young boys, each of the samplers in this book represents a year's work by a girl in her early teens or younger. All were accomplished sometime during the century or so that begins just before America's War for Independence and concludes not long after its War between the States. Some of these children were born into, or later married into, families whose members played important roles in America's past, but most are unknown. For them, their sampler has survived as the only remaining record of their lives. With that in mind as you look upon their work, you should be able to forgive them their displaced stitches, uneven borders, and a few visible waste knots.

The mottoes and verses they stitched resonate the stern judgments imposed upon them by religion and family. The row on row of tiny over-one stitches they crossed on uneven and tightly-woven linen testify equally to the acuity of their eyesight and their ability to accept the unyielding discipline of the task. And yet each child's individual spirit shows through, especially when you begin to duplicate her work. Stitch by stitch you will begin to sense the dimensions of that child's personality—stitches pulled with patience and impatience, a border that wavers with

A girl's skills, learned at school, increased her family's status as satirized in an etching dated 1809 by the British engraver, James Gillray.

resolve, charming asymmetries both intended and not, embellishments that emphasize her family name or enliven a favored motif.

Whether you chose only to admire this work, or to study it, or to replicate it exactly, you should never resist the temptation to think of the spirits that first stitched these pieces of history, as well as the role that these works played in their everyday lives.

WHAT ARE SAMPLERS AND WHY WERE THEY STITCHED?

Fragments of embroidered cloth have been discovered in tombs of early Egypt; however, the importance of needlework as a decorative and historical artifact does not emerge until the 11th century, when William of Normandy invaded Britain. It was then that the word "sampler" first entered the English vocabulary as the French word *essemplaire*. Even as William conquered the English in 1066 and made his native French the language of the elite in England, workers in the French town of Bayeux recorded his triumphs in one of history's most extraordinary commemorative tapestries. Though not an *essemplaire*, the Bayeux tapestry demonstrates the extraordinary skill of the people who worked it, and it reveals a great deal about daily life in the time during which it was stitched, as do the samplers in this book.

Over the years, the British adapted the French word to their own "exemplar" and then "examplar," before they eventually shortened the pronunciation and spelling to that of "sampler." Originally, the word was applied to a piece of decorative embroidery made as a reference pattern to be saved and copied by the more affluent women who held in high esteem the skills of needlework and sewing. Shortly before Shakespeare was born though (about 100 years before the Pilgrims set off for the New World), the meaning of the word began to change with the meaning of the work involved. By then, learning stitchery and alphabets had become part of the formal training for every young girl, not just those of the privileged classes. As a result, a "sampler" became more truly a sample of a girl's needlework skill.

Woven fabric. When the pieces in this book were stitched, weaving linen was a painstaking process done by hand with threads spun from flax. Linen made locally or in the home was called "tabby-weave" linen, and the tension in such pieces was usually loose and uneven. Young George Eisenbrey's sampler, which was stitched on 25-count linen (25 threads to the inch), is a good example of tabby-weave. On the other hand, if a girl was from a wealthy family, her parents purchased linens of a higher quality for her sampler. This finer linen had a higher thread count and was usually "evenweave," (woven with equal tension so that the number of threads to the inch was the same both horizontally and vertically). As examples, Dorothy Allen stitched her sampler on a relatively fine, 35-count evenweave and the last work in this book, the Drawstring Bag, was worked on unusually fine 50-count linen.

Until the early 18th century, linen was woven on looms only eight or nine inches wide. As a result, most old samplers are called "band" samplers because of their long, narrow shape.

Machine-woven, evenweave linen is preferred for stitching samplers today. However, to replicate an antique unevenweave so that the dimensions of a reproduction sampler match those of the original antique, a stitcher can draw out threads from the warp or woof of evenweave. The technique is described in the Appendix to this book.

In addition, the natural cream color of an original antique sampler's linen darkens almost as if it were dipped into coffee. The Appendix to this book also provides recipes using coffee or tea to dye modern, cream-colored linen in ways that will more nearly replicate the uneven tones of antique linen as commercially dyed "mocha" linen does not.

Alphabets. For practice, as well as for reference, samplers always contained uppercase letters and often lowercase, as well as the numbers one to nine.

"Who made the Scholar proud to show,/ The sampler worked to friend and foe./ And with instruction fonder grow?/ My Governess." This engraving and verse are from My Governess, *published in 1825.*

A young girl needed to practice and learn how to stitch her alphabet and numbers in order to mark the bed linen, bath linen, table linen and personal linen she also would be expected to sew. Customarily, she began preparing those items long before she was old enough to marry, so she embroidered her own initials on "upstairs" items, such as personal linen and clothing. After she married, however, the more valuable "downstairs" table linens, like the silverware, bore the initials of her married name. Consequently, the first sampler a girl stitched was usually a simple "marking" sampler which, in addition to helping her learn her alphabet, often reproduced a variety of styles of letters, (and, more rarely, decorative motifs, she fancied or inherited) so she could use the sampler as a record of letter-forms to copy later when needed. (Lydia Tyler's is one example of a skillful marking sampler.) Because most bed and table linen in those days all looked pretty much alike, each item had to be "marked." In addition to the proper initials, stitched numbers and letters identified a specific item and allowed linen to be rotated as used. Traditionally, such markings indicated the year the item was acquired, denoted the quality—as in *B* for "best"—and often showed the dimensions. To this day, the tradition of marking linen or clothing with initials or emblems continues with the monogramming of towels, fine handkerchiefs and custom-made shirts.

Motifs, mottoes and verses. In addition to those utilitarian aspects of a sampler, decorative motifs often added a purely aesthetic quality. Children often created motifs and borders that were inspired by the designs they witnessed around them in nature, in illustrated books, or in decorative carvings and fabrics. These motifs were usually flowers in traditional baskets, or vases, or in repeat borders. Often, too, they appear to have been simply some favorite objects: birds, a pet, occasionally a building but almost never a human figure.

Though British samplers were filled with large decorative designs, early colonial samplers, especially from the northern colonies, were dominated by alphabets; decoration was secondary. This was in keeping with the religious and social values of the environment in which they were created. In addition, American samplers often quoted from scripture, mottoes, or short verses to display the stitcher's devotion to duty, patience, and humility before God and parental authority. Still, the pure dedication, the disarmingly inventive details, and the occasional bright colors in early American samplers all demand appreciation and invite delight over and over again.

Dating and naming. An American sampler also commonly included the name and age of the girl who stitched it. Sometimes when the last one or two digits of the date are missing she probably had removed them later in her life because she did not want others to be able to calculate her age. The last digits of the year were not filled in until the sampler was completed. For that reason they may remain blank if the child died before she finished the work. Death at such an early age was not uncommon then, especially in the colonies of the New World and later on the frontier of the new republic.

In fact, the colonial custom of dating and naming a sampler appears to have been traced back to a whitework sampler stitched in 1610 by a girl named Ann Gower. Ann brought her sampler with her when she crossed the Atlantic to the Massachusetts Bay Colony with her husband, the future Governor Winthrop. Recognized as the oldest colonial sampler on record in America, Ann Gower's work established the tradition of attaching a name and a date to the important milestone that the stitching of a sampler represented in a young girl's life.

Preservation. Antique samplers that remain in good condition today do so because they were rarely framed. More commonly, a young girl would roll up her sampler on wooden or ivory pins and store it in a drawer, bringing it out only when asked to prove her skill, proper schooling, filial devotion, or eligibility for marriage. Though colors gradually faded if the

threads were exposed to light, they may be preserved on the back of the sampler or deduced by comparison with unfaded threads of the same period. Some natural dyes, especially blacks made from chestnuts, caused threads to disintegrate over time.

CHARACTERISTICS OF EARLY AMERICAN SAMPLERS

The differences between an English and an American sampler arise not so much from the nationality of the stitcher herself, as from the effect of social factors. Not the least of these was the difference in religious influence upon a child's upbringing. For example, young girls in England were more likely to stitch the sort of decorative embroidery worn in ceremonies conducted by the church or royalty, while young girls in certain American colonies had a more Puritanical upbringing which demanded more practical and less decorative skills. Since American girls concentrated more upon their alphabets, they had to make the lines of letters come out even within the borders, as type does. This required ingenuity. Sometimes they "adjusted" an otherwise symmetrical border. When they ran out of space, often they simply omitted letters, tucked a letter or the last word of a sentence above the line, narrowed the space between words, crowded their letters, or made them more compact by stitching over one thread instead of the usual two. If a line ran short, on the other hand, they often doubled letters to extend it, as Susana Bartholomew did by adding a second "W" to her name.

The oldest extant sampler stitched in this country is pictured at left. Loara Standish, the daughter of Miles Standish, worked it on tabby-weave in 1643, in the style of an English band sampler. Before she was twenty years old, Loara completed the stitching with two different weights of silk in various shades of green, cream, yellow, brown, buff and blue. Displayed in Pilgrim Hall in Plymouth Massachusetts, it bears both her name and a verse.

In the American colonies and the early years of the republic, needlework was the common denominator of all schooling for girls. Young men were far more likely than girls to be taught Math, Reading and Writing. Young girls were taught either by their mothers and sisters at home, or else at a Dame School. Families that could afford it sent older daughters to a boarding or day school. It was in these types of schooling that the distinguishable form of American samplers evolved, hence the phrase "schoolgirl sampler."

Distinctive ways of stitching alphabets and decorative motifs were passed down from mother to daughter or perpetuated by schools. Dame Schools often were established by a girl or widow who taught the youngest girls from the village or neighborhood several mornings or afternoons each week, in exchange for money, firewood or whatever other bargain might have been struck. Girls would be taught manners, how to run a household, and how to do domestic needlework. (Though it is very rare, occasionally a boy was forced to attend a school with the girls if he had angered his parents or disgraced them to the extent that they felt he needed to learn patience or self-discipline. One of the two boy's samplers in this book, George Eisenbrey's, was stitched for this reason. Julian Chamberlain's, however, was stitched at home to occupy him during an illness.)

By examining an antique sampler closely it is often possible to guess how the child was schooled. Girls whose parents had the means to send them to a formal school usually stitched their samplers not only on large pieces of imported linen, but also with as much thread as was needed in the colors they chose. Also, a sampler that employs a variety of decorative stitches in addition to cross stitch usually indicates formal training. Many schools for girls required their students to follow a discernable style or include a "signature" motif, as the sampler in this book by Mary Carpenter demonstrates. If a child were taught to stitch by a governess or in a school she might identify her teacher by stitching her full name, or more commonly, include only the initials somewhere on

the piece, as both Polly Daggett and Lydia Tyler did.

Many of the formal schools were denominational. The Moravians, for example, taught boys and girls as equals from the time their church was established in Pennsylvania in 1741. They are, perhaps, the only group in America to have done this in their day, and they are represented in this book by Sophia Elizabeth Kummer's simple prayer. Samplers stitched by girls sent to Quaker schools are also represented by Hannah Atkins, among others.

Children of families who could not afford to send their girls away for formal schooling also reveal their social or economic status in their samplers. For one thing, they are more likely to work on homespun tabby-weave. For another, they switch colors with charming eccentricity as they use up whatever threads are available in their mothers' sewing boxes. Mary Mosely, for example, even stitched half a letter in one color and the other half in another. Or witness the sampler of Sophia Waters, where, in the midst of an all-brown piece, there sits a delightful little bit of blue in the "on" of Bennington.

After the early 1700s, pattern books were more readily available and became another source of recognizable uniformity. Not many are left in existence today because of the practice of "pricking" that came into popularity. Pricking was a new way of transferring the desired design to a piece of cloth. A series of small pin pricks was made in the letter of whatever was being copied. When that was placed over the cloth, ashes from the fireplace were lightly sifted over this. When the book was removed, a line of sooty dots remained to be stitched over. Naturally, after many prickings, the books fell apart.

English children often put crowns on their samplers, sometimes with letters over them indicating a rank of nobility. It seems ironic to see crowns on American samplers, particularly around the time of the Revolution. The convention was taken from a printer's mark. To fill in a space in the pattern book, a printer would place a crown on the page and the

While Thomas Jefferson's daughter, Martha, was away at school, he wrote to her as follows in 1787...

In the country life of America there are many moments when a woman can have recourse to nothing but her needle for employment. (Editor's note: by "employment" he meant useful activity or a pastime, not a way to earn money.) *In a dull company and in dull weather for instance. It is ill manners to read; it is ill manners to leave them; no card playing there among genteel people; that is abandoned to blackguards. The needle is then a valuable resource. Besides without knowing how to use it herself, how can the mistress of a family direct the works of her servants?*

...and again, three years later:

How are you occupied? ...How many pages a day you read in Don Quixot [sic]? *How far are you advanced in him. Whether you repeat a Grammar lesson every day? What else you read? How many hours a day you sew? Whether you have an opportunity of continuing your music? Whether you know how to make a pudding yet, to cut out a beef steak, to sow spinach or to set a hen?...*

child copying a row would also include the crown in her work. American "crowns" have no letters surrounding them to indicate rank. Sophia Waters used one in her sampler in 1803.

Stitching mistakes. Though many American girls were extraordinarily skillful stitchers, the rule most followed seems to have been: "Whatever happens, keep going at all costs." They tended to be especially sloppy about stitching over two threads, sometimes making one or three instead, and tangled backs abound.

The children who stitched the samplers in this book followed few rules and merrily carried threads from letter to letter, word to word, and line to line whenever it suited them. Proper English girls knotted and trimmed their thread and began anew if they had to skip more than a few linen threads before starting a new stitch, but American girls tended to drag their threads across the back as far as needed to start the next stitch. In antique American samplers it is also not unusual to see places where the linen was cut accidentally when the silk threads were snipped, to remove a stitching mistake, perhaps, then the cut was stitched over thickly to cover it.

The sampler charts provided in this book replicate the mistakes in the original samplers, including uncrossed and broken threads. Stitchery charts, however, cannot graph the whimsical changes in the direction with which a child crosses her stitches. If you give any young child a piece of fabric, a needle and a pattern, then show her how a cross stitch is made, she probably would be able to execute simple designs. Still, she will rarely cross each stitch in the same direction. Children in the 18th and mid-19th century were no different. Only Eliza Hall, age seven, and Rachel Ellicott, age eleven, crossed the majority of their stitches in the same direction. These two girls were definitely in the minority.

NEEDLE WORK.

EMBROID'RY, flowers, and Plain-work too
Th'docile maiden shews to view;
In ev'ry branch a scholar true

THE SCHOOL-GIRL!

A page from a book published in London, entitled The School-Girl *in 1820, portrays how sternly children were judged by the quality of their stitchery then.*

Those who choose to stitch an accurate replica of an antique sampler should mix their crossings. Though neatness and consistency may be worthy objectives in many pursuits, a truly authentic-looking sampler requires that the stitcher abandon perfection.

Alphabet variations. Most young girls worked from the top, and stitched one or more alphabets, sometimes in different lettering or stitches. Occasionally, they fashioned variations in alphabets within the same sampler. Sometimes a sampler with varying stitches and styles of alphabets reveals that the child was preserving conventions established in samplers wrought by her mother and grandmother; other times, it simply repeats mistakes. Rachel Ellicott, for example, copied some of her alphabets passed down through two generations. One alphabet omitted some letters that were little used in earlier days and Rachel dutifully replicated the omission.

Designs. When they finished their alphabets, stitchers might introduce design motifs, free-standing or worked into borders. American girls tended to show their independence of mind and inventive imaginations most noticeably when they created motifs such as family possessions, pets, birds, or trees of all descriptions. (In her sampler, Mary Robinson stitched a robin just above her name.) Sometimes a particular object of affection—a cat, or trees or flowers—would dwarf other images of houses or people. These images and their proportions are both charming and valuable as a true child's-eye view of their world. Buildings were also sometimes stitched onto the work, and historians have found samplers helpful in picturing houses and public buildings which may have been destroyed along the way. In some instances, the building may still exist, though its surroundings have changed.

Verses and sayings. Some of the text found in antique American samplers seems terribly sad to modern readers. They show not only the weight of the stern religious duty, but also the sense of impending judgment felt by the children of the time as well as how soon they expected to be released from life to join the Lord. Children also created or copied verses that spoke of their duty to their parents, the virtue of industry, or the fickleness of love. Two of the samplers in this book, those by Maria Revere Curtis, who was Paul Revere's great-granddaughter, and Hannah Atkins, a Quaker from Cape Cod, used the same verse. They were born within a few years of each other and lived only 90 miles apart. A representative sampling of verses and mottoes from old samplers are provided in the Appendix to this book.

Map Samplers. About 1770, an English printer named John Spilsbury perfected a way of reproducing the outlines of a map on light-colored cloth or satin. These outlines invited tracing in cross stitch as a means of teaching geography in schools where children learned stitchery. In general, though, American map samplers were created freehand, often with clever or amusing results.

Tambour work. Intricate designs to be chain-stitched into the sampler were drawn or traced onto the fabric, usually with a pencil. Surviving antique samplers that reveal portions of the design which teachers may have sketched

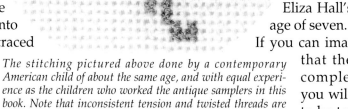

The stitching pictured above done by a contemporary American child of about the same age, and with equal experience as the children who worked the antique samplers in this book. Note that inconsistent tension and twisted threads are not unique to time or place; nor is the charm of the effort.

(but the children did not complete) confirm this technique. The stitcher places the portion of the fabric with the penciled design into a hoop. She works the design with fine, small chain stitches by catching her threads with a very small hook resembling a superfine crochet hook. If the linen threads are counted while the stitching is done, the resulting stitches look machine stitched. In this collection, Joann Isabella Gibbs' sampler includes two tambour-work motifs.

Mourning samplers. Usually a mourning sampler commemorated the death of someone in the family. Life spans were short in those days, and children often died at an especially young age. This helps account for the large number of memorial samplers that have survived. Typically these picture willow trees and black coffins along with the name and age of a lost sibling. The ultimate act of mourning for a

stitcher was to stitch a lock of her own hair into the sampler somewhere. This practice was not common, however, so such samplers are rare.

In this collection, the sampler stitched by Martha and Mary Fitzhugh is a genealogical record that became a mourning sampler. Poor Martha Fitzhugh died at age seven while working on this piece which records the wedding and birth dates of family members, then commemorates the death of two of her sisters. At least one other member of the family picked up the piece to finish it in the ensuing years.

A final word. As you savor the work in this collection, remember how young many of these children were when they had to prove themselves by working a sampler. Avoid passing judgment upon what might appear to be misspellings or omissions from the alphabets. The lowercase letter "s" still looked like an "f" until well after the American Revolution, as shown in the unusually skillful alphabet stitched by Fanny Mots in 1792 at the age of eleven. In Dorothy Allen's simple "samplar" stitched in 1732, there is no "J" in the uppercase alphabet, because that letter was not in use at the time. And witness Eliza Hall's exquisite work at the age of seven.

If you can imagine the dutiful hours that these children put into completing their samplers, you will find it impossible not to be touched by the dropped stitches, the crooked lines, and the letters left out only to be later tucked in above their proper place in line. None of these girls could have imagined that their work would survive to be displayed in museums and appreciated 250 years later by needleworkers, scholars, and collectors.

Throughout the ages, however tedious or dark, the impulse to decorate and to beautify has remained a triumph of the human spirit. As you examine the work reproduced in these pages, always keep in mind that the voices of these children are speaking to you through their embroidery. If you can do this, then you will come to appreciate them as individuals as much—or maybe more—for their mistakes as for their facility, their designs or occasionally famous names. And if you should choose a sampler to duplicate, you will do honor to the child whose original stitches represented a milestone in her young life.

THE SAMPLERS

DOROTHY ALLEN

A rare miniature band sampler stitched
by Ethan Allen's cousin.

 The genealogical evidence available suggests that the twenty-four-year-old woman who stitched this "samplar" in 1732 was a first cousin of Revolutionary War hero Ethan Allen, who led Vermont's legendary Green Mountain Boys in the capture of Fort Ticonderoga from the British in 1775.

Her "band" of fabric appears to have come from the type of loom used in the 16th and 17th centuries which could not weave fabric more than nine inches wide. Rather than arrange her numerals in a straight line, as was common, she used some in the date and in her age, then fitted a 5 and a 6 among her decorative motifs. It was not uncommon in samplers, even up to 1750, to omit the letters *U* and *J* and spell sampler *samplar*, as she did.

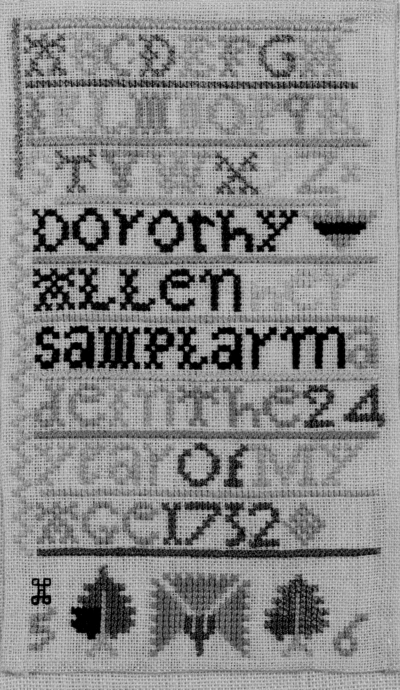

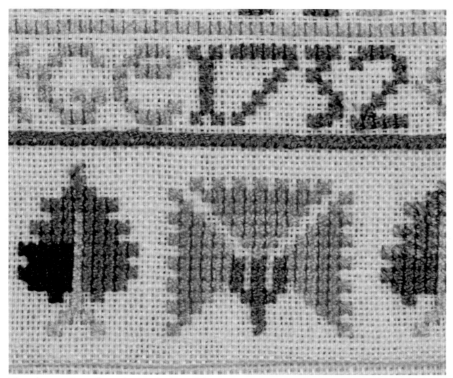

Dorothy was brought up in the shadow of the Green Mountains of Vermont, which was then part of New York State. No wonder she chose symbols from nature such as trees and a wild turkey.

With Yankee ingenuity, she kept her lower-case letters all the same height.

DIRECTIONS

Work with one strand of Au Ver a Soie® silk unless otherwise specified. (One strand is equal in thickness to two strands of DMC floss.)

Near the bottom, work the group of boxes that are located over the numeral **5** in four-sided stitch with a single strand of #1425 navy, except for the bottom two boxes, which are worked with two strands.

DOROTHY ALLEN
(3⅞ x 6½ inches)

Dorothy completed this sampler when she was 24 years old—more than twice the average age of children who stitched samplers 250 years ago. Though she was not an accomplished needlewoman, the color and sheen of the silk threads she chose to use on a light background capture the eye. When you see the original, it is hard to believe it was worked before America's war for independence.

This is a band sampler in miniature size. Until the early 18th century, the width that linen could be woven was limited by the width of narrow looms. For that reason, the older samplers, especially English ones, were stitched on relatively long, narrow bands of linen. The original size of the linen on which Dorothy stitched measured 3⅞ x 6½ inches, including ⅛-inch hems on all four sides. This small size is suited to experimentation with unfamiliar stitches; the design size measures only 3½ inches across.

The General Instructions in the Appendix show how to find the starting point and work the stitches.

MATERIALS
9⅞ x 12½ inches of 35-count ivory linen, dyed with the #1 Tea recipe (see Appendix); Au Ver a Soie® silk as shown in the Chart Key (note that some stitches are blended); size 26 tapestry needle.

C H A R T	K E Y	
SYMBOL	Au Ver a Soie®	COLOR
O	1814	med. dk. green
▼	1745	lt. slate blue
ว	1732	gray
z	4113	rosy brown
L	2231, 2234	lt. gold/gold blend
✳	2223	green-gold
<	3832	tan
K	3723	green
E	3721	lightest green
‖	1714, 1745	blue/slate blue, blend
•	3831	lt. tan, 1 str.
φ	3426	darkest green
X	3836	dk. brown
	1425	navy: 4-sided st.
■	1744	slate blue

Dorothy was not a poor speller at 24 years of age; in the mid-18th century, variant spellings were both common and accepted.

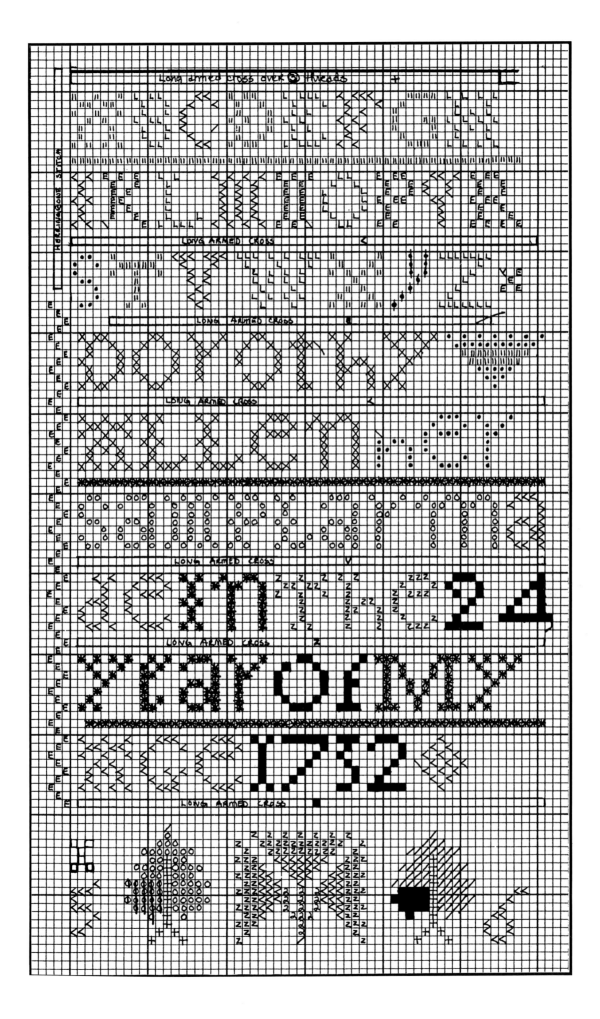

POLLY DAGGETT

Legendary Revolutionary War heroine from Martha's Vineyard.

Mary Daggett, known affectionately as Polly, was born in 1760 in the town of Holmes Hole (now Vineyard Haven) on the seafaring island of Martha's Vineyard. When she was not yet fifteen, a British ship, HMS *Unicorn*, put into the harbor one morning. Its captain, having observed a liberty pole the islanders had erected on a hill as a monument to their independence, demanded that they deliver it to his ship by the next day as a replacement spar. Legend has it that Polly and two of her friends drilled holes into the pole that night, packed them with gunpowder, and blew it to splinters.

At nineteen, Polly married a master mariner named Peleg Hillman, who was Quartermaster of the privateer *Oliver Cromwell*. She divorced him ten years later. Before she died at a ripe old age, "Aunt Polly" became much beloved by the children in the island village of Tisbury.

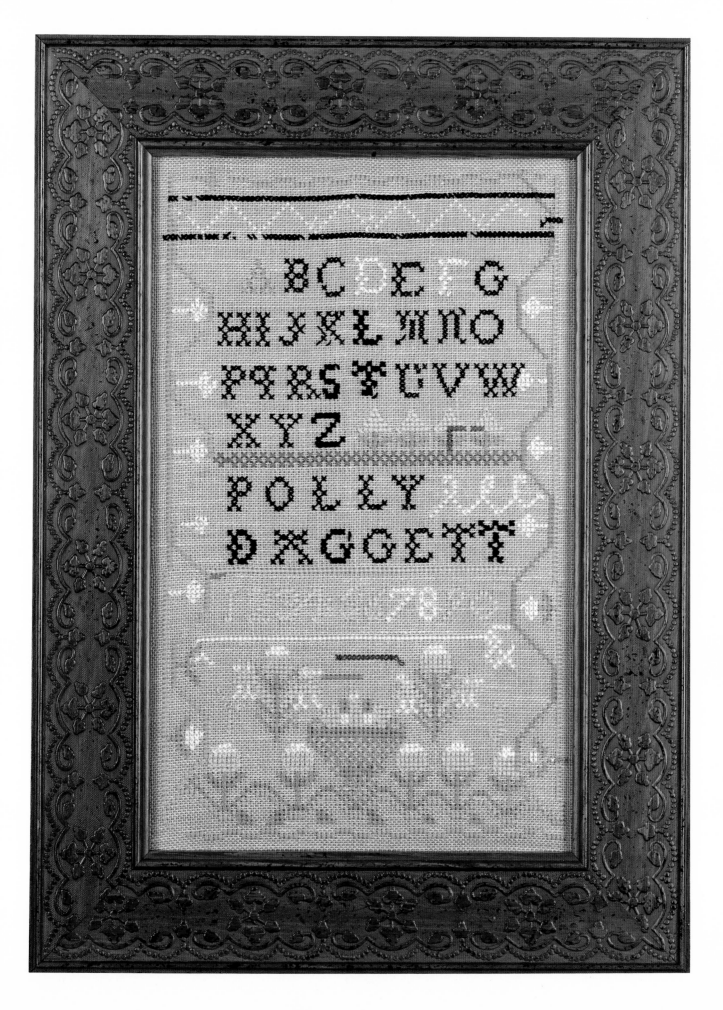

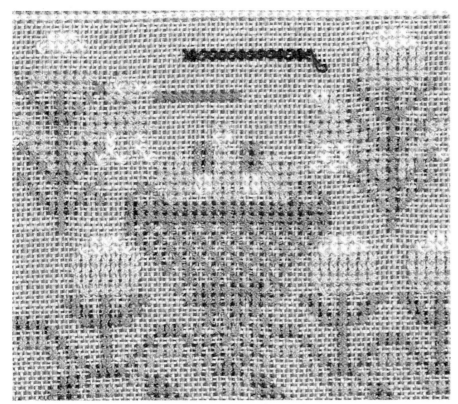

The bountiful basket is a design motif found in many decorative media of the period including wall stencils, theorem painting (stenciling on velvet), piecework, and appliqué.

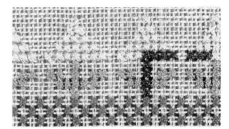

These stylized trees are not difficult to stitch. They resemble the conifers she saw on her island home.

POLLY DAGGETT
(7 x 11 ¼ inches)

Although there is no way of knowing for sure how old Polly was, most children stitched their samplers at about age ten. If she did, she stitched this sampler in 1770, the same year that British troops fired into a mob in Boston on the evening of March 5th—a politically inflammatory event that Paul Revere dramatized in his etching *The Boston Massacre.*

Polly's uncluttered work seems to reflect her simple island upbringing. The canvas is probably a homespun tabby-weave linen, unusual for the white flecks in it. She chose earthy colors—greens, khakis, golds, and black—all of which can be created in a home dye pot. Note the charming effect of the plain white yarn (which originally was light pink).

By the looks of it, Polly was given more to determined action than fussy stitching. Her uppercase alphabet is bold but not very straight. She varied the thickness of her threads arbitrarily, as if compelled to use whatever thickness was available to

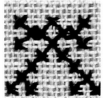 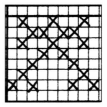

Polly chose an antique font to celebrate the letter **A** in her name. The cross normally found inside the letter appears across the top.

her as she worked on her letters day by day. Her side borders tend to wander, waver, and spread out here and there. All this must have distressed her teacher, whom Polly identified by her initials on either side near the bottom—**A** in green, and **J** in a color almost lost in the background.

The General Instructions in the Appendix show how to find the starting point and work the stitches.

MATERIALS
13 x 17 inches of 25-count cream linen, dyed with the #2 Coffee recipe (see Appendix); DMC embroidery floss as shown in the Chart Key (note variations in the number of strands of floss used for some colors); size 24 tapestry needle.

DIRECTIONS
When working this sampler note that Polly frequently displaced stitches by crossing incorrect threads in the linen. She used cross stitch with some variations in thread thickness, as noted in the Chart Key. When working the dividing bands above and below the numbers, pull the threads tight as Polly did in her original work. If you decide to hem the finished piece as shown in the photograph on the previous page, count 15 threads from the finished stitching toward the edges of the linen and trim it all around. Fold the fabric under at the eighth thread and backstitch in about six threads from the edge all the way around. The linen thread used for hemming should match the linen of the sampler, so draw out the longest linen threads from the scrap fabric you trimmed off.

CHART KEY		
SYMBOL	DMC #	COLOR
■	370	khaki
6	371	khaki
◢	372	khaki
O	502	blue-green
B	927	slate blue
U	520	dk. blue-green
T E	834	dirty gold, 4 str.
A	368	apple green
―	3011	green
L Z	613	tan: Medici yarn, 1 str.
•	3046	bright gold
n	920	orange
C	336	navy
K	543	ivory, 4 str.
X ✳	310	black, 2 str., 4 str.

MARY HILL

Upside down numbers—a secret wartime code or the work of her sister?

 She was only eight or nine years old in 1773 when the Boston Tea Party came to symbolize the colonies' anger toward England's tax on their daily tea. It is tempting to imagine that the apparently random letters strung together, sometimes upside down, with omissions, variant spellings, and a backwards-tailing *y*, were some sort of code devised by radical revolutionaries in her Warwick, Rhode Island, family. On the other hand, a sibling may also have worked on the sampler and simply turned her sister's project upside down to distinguish her own handiwork. Clearly there was no money to buy a bigger piece of imported, 50-count linen, but Mary managed to get as much practice out of her three- by six-inch sampler as most colonial girls got out of their larger canvases. Whatever the reason for her charming jumble, the personality revealed in this little sampler makes it a delightful conversation piece.

Collection of Museum of Fine Arts, Boston, Massachusetts.

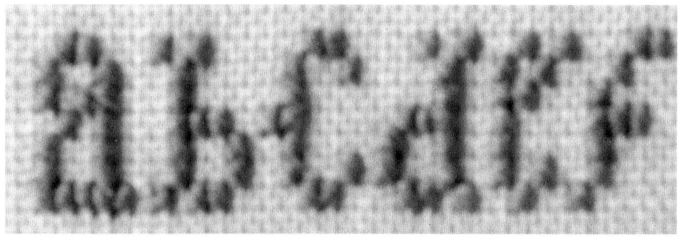

One of the reasons for creating a sampler is to learn to form the letters of an alphabet with stitches. Making all the letters uniform in height and in proportion to each other is the biggest challenge. The top alphabet in

Mary's sampler is a beautiful example of mid-17th century lettering style. The first five letters are especially typical of this period and are a pleasure to stitch.

MARY HILL
(6 x 3 inches)

Mary chose fairly bright colors, especially the reds in the top alphabet. The natural, 50-count fabric she worked on has turned a beautiful beige over the years. The decorative effect is most inviting. It is made even more charming by the hodgepodge of letters and numbers. There seems to be neither rhyme, nor reason to most of the second and third lines except for the date at the end of the third. It appears almost as if she practiced only the letters she liked.

The straightforward verse that occupies the fourth, fifth, and part of the sixth lines reads like one unbroken word, so economically did she employ her allotted space. The whimsical tail on the lower-case **Y** in **MARY** and **MY NAME** slants the wrong way, but then it switches back correctly in **MY NEDLE**.

It is possible that she may have stitched some sort of code into her sampler. This notion is derived from the three sets of numbers stitched upside down and the three letters executed in unbelievably meticulous eyelet stitches, two of which are upside down as well. It is also possible that a sibling turned it upside down to work on the same piece.

The General Instructions in the Appendix show how to find the starting point and work the stitches.

Her eyelet stitches are remarkably uniform and neatly stitched. They are particularly difficult to execute on linen as tightly woven as the 50-count ground she worked on.

MATERIALS
12 x 9 inches of 50-count ivory linen; DMC embroidery floss as shown in the Chart Key (note use of one to four strands); size 26 tapestry needle.

DIRECTIONS
The eyelet stitches are made with one strand on 50-count weave and may require the use of a magnifying glass. Near the end of the top row the letters that look like a stylized **U** and an unfinished **W** are formed with a backstitch between each cross stitch.

 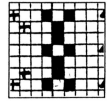

Mary's sister may have had a hand in this sampler. Possibly for that reason Mary was determined to impress upon anyone who saw it that her needle did the work. She emphasized the first person singular in her verse with thread so thick that the I literally stands out.

This spelling of "needle" may have been an accepted variant in the 18th century, but the letters in the entire line had to be stitched so closely together to get all the words in, one is tempted to imagine that she dropped the second e to save space.

Use one strand for the eyelets and the letters **Z** and **D** in the third row, three strands for the **5** in the second row, and four strands for her **I**.

CHART KEY		
SYMBOL	**DMC #**	**COLOR**
X	926	slate blue
O	347	red
✳	734	olive green
✚ ‖ ■	407	rose: 1 str., 2 str., 3 str.
V	927	lt. slate blue
I	644	lt. beige
•	504	lightest blue-green
U	613	beige
L	3047	lightest yellow
✚ ■	371	green: 1 str., 4 str.
e	334	blue
▲	934	darkest green
Z	310	black

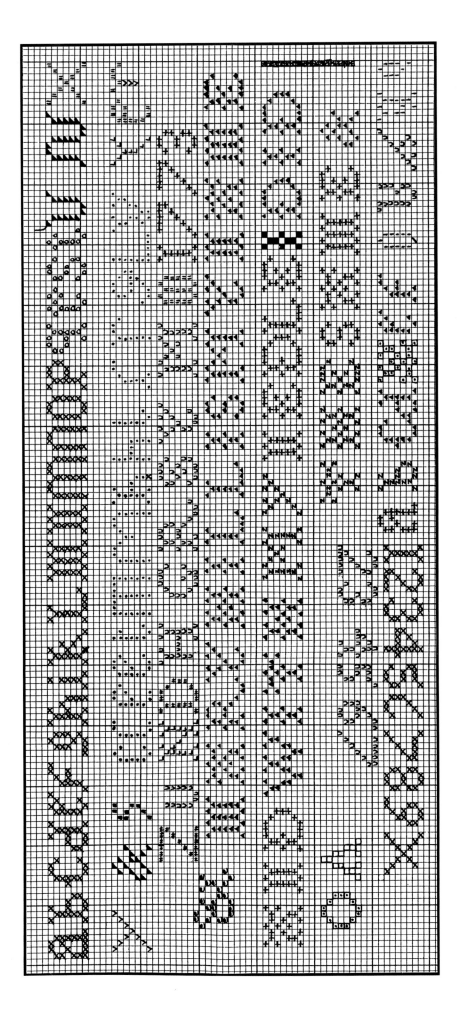

FANNY MOTS

Her unpuritanical taste in color shows up in the pink floral borders.

 Fanny's background is a mystery. Though she probably came from a town north of Boston, the official registries of births in Massachusetts do not show a child by that name to have been born in 1781. It is possible that she was named for a sibling: The birth of a Fanny Mots was registered in the town of Lynnfield, but that child died when she was only nine months old. It was common then to give a newborn the same name as a sibling or other relative that had died in infancy.

Fanny must have worked her sampler under the stern eye of a teacher because neither she nor her mother is likely to have chosen the time-consuming eyelet stitch worked over only one thread instead of the usual two. But with patience and fairly good eyesight, this piece will reward you for the many pleasant hours devoted to it.

Collection of Essex Institute, Salem, Massachusetts.

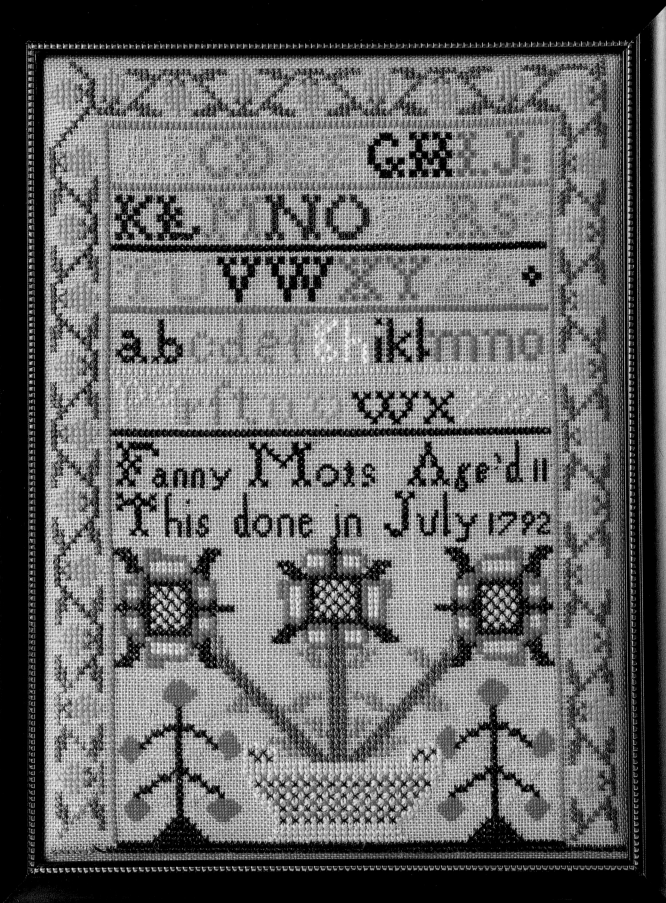

Fanny's sampler reveals a cosmopolitan influence in her choice of a gay pink for the floral borders and in bold design, notably the three, large elaborate flowers. As shown in the left flower, above, she used only one strand for the black lattice work to replicate the delicate centers of real flowers.

FANNY MOTS
(7⅝ x 10 inches)

Fanny's sampler has been preserved in excellent condition at the Essex Institute in Salem, Massachusetts. When you look at her work, your eyes are drawn immediately to the side flowers, which droop noticeably. Perhaps she was anxious to finish and, in her haste, pulled the stitches on the side flowers too tightly, making them appear to sag over the berries. Of course, tension cannot be charted, but you can try to reproduce the same effect if you like by tightening your stitches there too.

The General Instructions in the Appendix show how to find the starting point and work the individual stitches.

MATERIALS
13⅝ x 16 inches of 25-count mocha linen, dyed with the #2 Coffee recipe (see Appendix); DMC embroidery floss as shown in the Chart Key (note that the symbols change for single vs. double-strand in #310 and #738); size 24 tapestry needle.

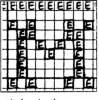

Fanny worked her eyelet stitches in the uppercase letters over two threads, not four.

DIRECTIONS
Work this sampler with both one and two strands of floss as shown in the stitching chart and Chart Key. Stitch the uppercase alphabet in an eyelet stitch worked over two threads instead of the usual four. This is not difficult, but it does require patience. Where the chart indicates stitches over one thread instead of the usual two, use only one strand of floss.

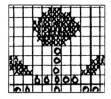

She worked the oversized berries on the two trees with one strand over one thread.

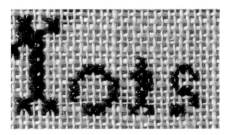

She left some stitches unfinished and, like anyone else, made some mistakes. They are all charted to allow authentic reproduction.

Use #918 floss to stitch the berries and #524 for the leaves. Stitch the lowercase letters of the words and the date in #310. Backstitch the border in two different colors (they are indicated by a broken line for the lighter #501, and a solid, darker line for #823). This method of working the border duplicates the hemstitch used on the original sampler. Work these stitches in the center of the two-stitch square, but pull them slightly tighter to reproduce the look of Fanny's original. There are three, ¼-inch, outer borders with the bottom remaining only a selvage edge under the final row of stitching.

CHART KEY		
SYMBOL	**DMC #**	**COLOR**
6	223	med. pink
●	501	dk. blue-green; b.s. border = broken line
V	502	med. blue-green
O	823	navy: b.s. border = heavy black line
3	939	dk. navy
Λ	500	dk. blue-green
⌐	834	lt. yellow-green
◰ ▨	918	rust, berries
X ▮ ✳	310	black: 1 str., 1 str. for lowercase letters, 2 str.
9	524	lt. green for small leaves with berries
C	841	lt. beige-brown
+	840	med. beige-brown
5 8	738	cream, 1 str., 2 str.
K	3047	pale yellow
●	924	teal blue
E	370	olive green
=	301	bright rust

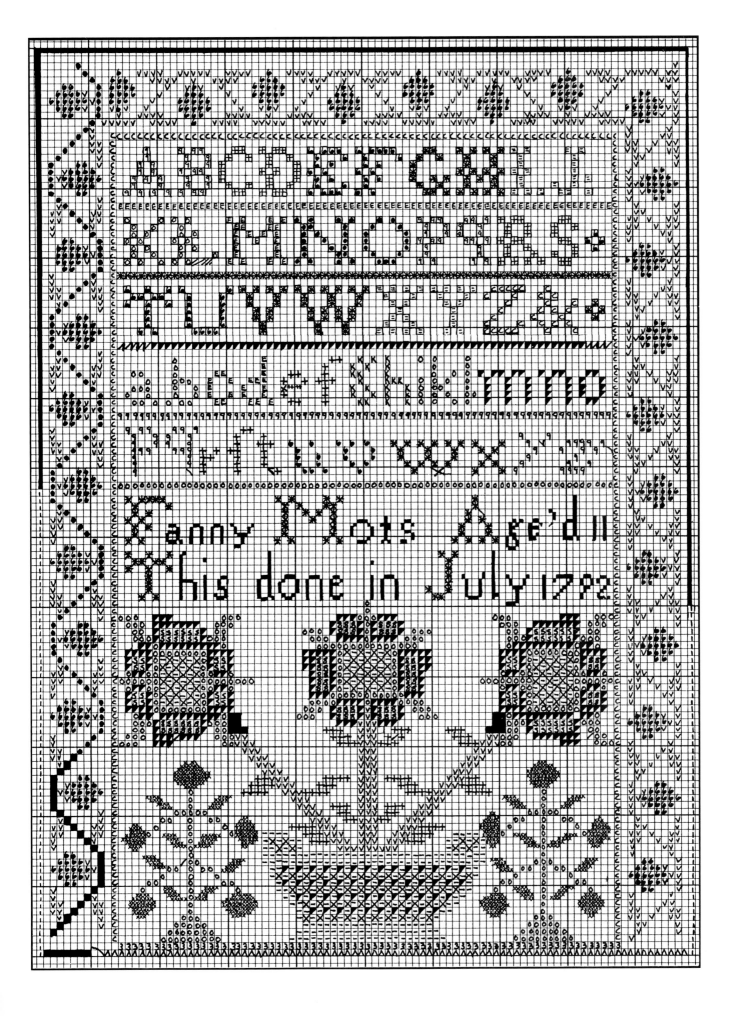

MARY MOSELY

Many color changes show Mary's need to use whatever thread was available.

Mary Mosely was born in 1784. She was the daughter of Captain Joseph Mosely, who sailed the ship *Enterprise* out of Salem, Massachusetts. She stitched her sampler in 1792 at the age of eight, probably at a dame school. Frequent color changes in the top two alphabets suggest to us how precious her limited supply of thread may have been. The beautiful mauve in the letter *D* done in eyelet stitch, for example, is seen nowhere else in the sampler.

Mary also tried stitching over one thread in her numerals at the bottom of her piece. Notice the backward *s* border beside the numerals. Small slips in the stitching of her vital information are included in our chart just as Mary stitched them.

Collection of Essex Institute, Salem, Massachusetts.

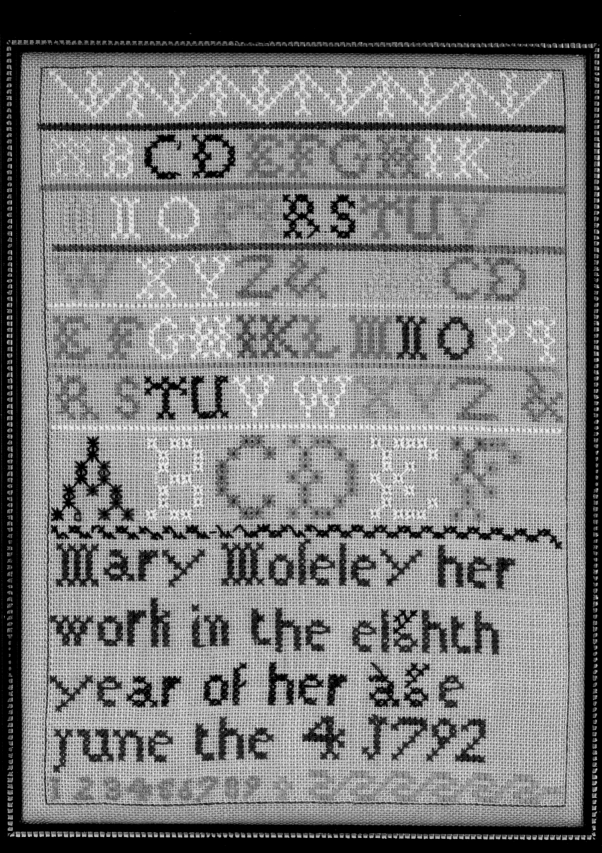

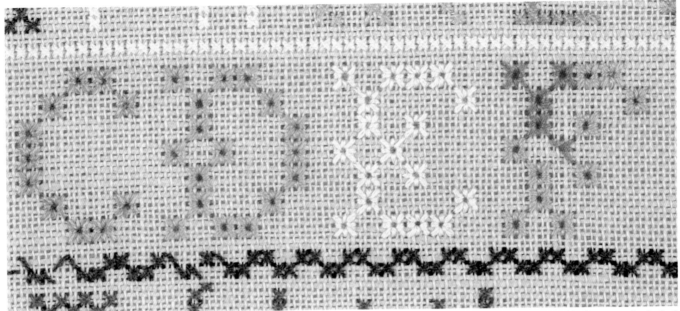

Mary used the eyelet stitch for one alphabet, but the small size of her cloth limited her to six letters. Thread, probably from her mother's sewing box, was at a premium, and so used sparingly. Note that she worked the F in two different colors, probably because she lacked enough of one color.

MARY MOSELY
(7⅝ x 10 inches)

Mary was not the most careful of stitchers, yet her piece speaks with a charm all its own. Her top two alphabets have omitted the letter **J**. Obviously, the undulating border beneath her eyelet alphabet was not stitched with great enthusiasm. Mary also seemed to have trouble keeping her words in a straight line in the first two lines of her verse (notice **Mary** and **work in**). By the third line she had corrected her uneven stitching and finished her sampler rather well with the exception of the numeral **5** which looks more like a misshapen 6. Her sampler gives the stitcher a chance to practice the eyelet stitch and cross stitch over one thread.

MATERIALS

13⅝ x 16 inches of 25-count mocha linen, dyed with the #2 Coffee recipe (see Appendix); DMC embroidery floss as shown in the Chart Key (note variations in number of strands); size 24 tapestry needle.

DIRECTIONS

Work the fourth dividing band over two threads across the stitch, but only one thread in height, in effect making

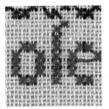

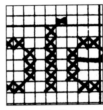

Sampler makers used a printer's S to save space well into the 1800s. Mary used it in her last name in this piece.

it a half cross stitch. Work the right-hand side with a single strand of floss. Use two strands for the left side.

Slashes in either direction or straight stitches show disintegrating or uncrossed threads and are stitched in the color you are currently using. For example, work the dividing band under the eyelet-stitch letters in #500.

The original sampler has 4¼-inch borders. Backstitch the border in #924. This duplicates the hemstitch on the original sampler. Pulling these stitches tighter will more closely approximate Mary's stitching.

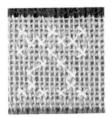

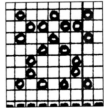

*Mary worked the first **A** in her alphabet with only one strand and the second with two strands. Perhaps she wanted one to stand out.*

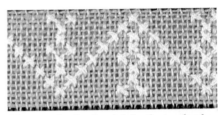

Mary used a lovely pink in the top border. Daylight has since faded it, but its original color still shows on the back of the sampler.

CHART KEY		
SYMBOL	**DMC #**	**COLOR**
●	3047/712	lt. gold-yellow/cream
X	924	teal blue
K	500	darkest green
–	301	rust
c	524	lt. green
3	841	med. brown
6	839	brown
+	931/813	slate blue/bright blue
V	3064	lt. rust
▮	975/301	lt. orange/rust: over 1 thread
E	975	lt. orange
O	3047	lt. gold-yellow, 1 str.
■	926/927	slate blue/lt. slate
⧄	316	mauve
	924	b.s. in teal blue for border

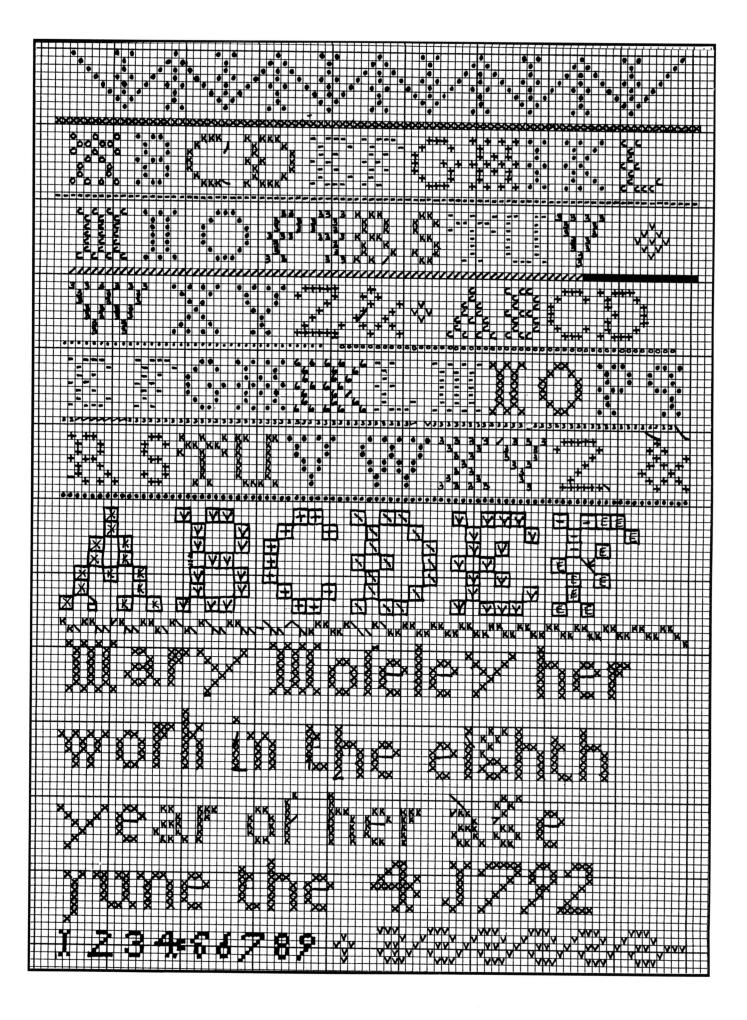

LYDIA TYLER

When This You See Remember Me— words stitched nearly 200 years ago.

 Lydia was a Massachusetts native, born to Jacob and Ruth Tyler of Methuen in 1787. Between the ages of nine and ten, Lydia studied her ABCs and stitchery at the home of Miss Sally Flint of Shrewsbury, who ran one of the small dame schools common in those days. Lydia must have boarded with Miss Flint because the two towns are too far apart to commute, and the Tylers could not have afforded a private tutor in residence.

Lydia married Jesse Clark of Tewksbury, Massachusetts, when she reached twenty-one. Only eight years later, after bearing two children, she succumbed to "consumption," a term used then to identify fatal sicknesses of unknown origin, often pneumonia.

Lydia Tyler Was
Born On Monday June The 25
1787 This Work I Wrought
When At School To Mifs Salt
Flint In The Year 1797 When
This You See Remember Me

"When This You See Remember Me." Is that not what every stitcher hopes for when working on a piece of decorative needlework? Lydia placed periods between the words—for emphasis, perhaps?

LYDIA TYLER
(11¾ x 9¼ inches)

A schoolgirl's marking sampler, like Lydia's, was a vehicle for mastering letter styles that she would use throughout her life to monogram linens. Although many girls worked their teacher's initials into their samplers, very few revealed their teacher's name, as Lydia did.

The General Instructions in the Appendix show how to find the starting point and work the stitches.

MATERIALS
17¾ x 15¼ inches of 25-count natural linen dyed with the #2 Coffee recipe (dye the sampler *after* the stitching is completed to make it look exactly as it does today, although this will render the stitching much less legible); DMC embroidery floss as shown in the Chart Key (note that #420 is worked with one strand); size 24 tapestry needle.

DIRECTIONS
Work this marking sampler with two strands except for the **Q** in #420, and entirely in cross stitch except for the sawtooth border. It will be easier to work the first line of the sampler, at least, before working the top border. After working the first **A** in the upper left corner, locate the bottom of the border by counting up seven stitches (each stitch over two threads) from the top left stitch on the **A**. From there you will work the longest thread in the second triangle of the sawtooth border. Start stitching the first triangle directly in line with the beginning of the first dividing band and end the border even with the last stitch of the same band.

Satin stitch the sawtooth border. Work it over one stitch for the width of the border. For the depth of each triangular segment, work over one thread progressing to six threads.

CHART KEY		
SYMBOL	**DMC #**	**COLOR**
O S	420	sand: 2 str., 1 str.
◢	434	brown
X	926	slate blue
+	3052	green
■	310	black
♯	833	gold
9	939	dk. navy
8	644	very lt. beige
6	613	tan
E	642	lt. beige
=	640	beige
•	747	lt. blue
	3012	lt. green, band only

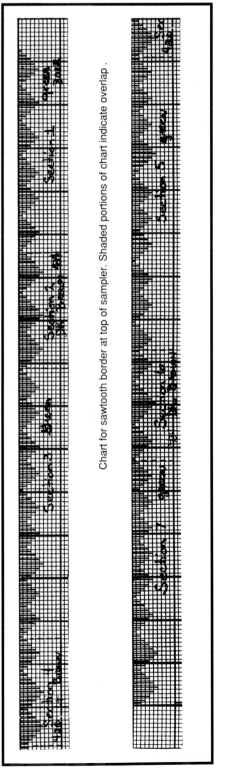

Chart for sawtooth border at top of sampler. Shaded portions of chart indicate overlap.

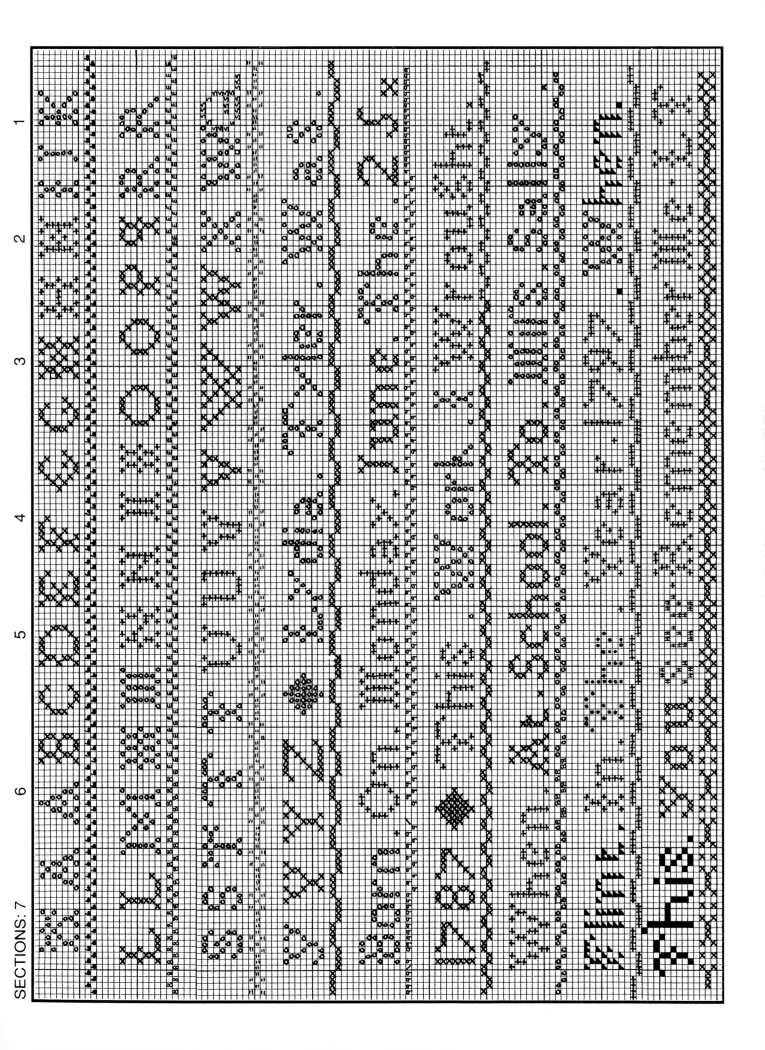

THANKFUL DAVIS

A seaside girl who used colors from a local dye pot and plenty of ingenuity.

She was born on March 5, 1787, near the Woods Hole section of Falmouth on Cape Cod, Massachusetts, and completed this simple yet whimsical sampler when she was thirteen years old. She waited until she was thirty-one to marry Job Gorham of Barnstable. They settled on Martha's Vineyard and had three children.

Thankful's colors are not vivid, which suggests that the threads were probably dyed at home rather than imported. She displays her ingenuity in many ways: She breaks her border when it doesn't work out right, and she uses thick threads or thin ones, whichever was available. Cleverly, she works the flower tops in *three* strands of white to make them stand out. She refers to herself as both *her* and *hur*. Perhaps she was an uncertain speller who wanted to cover both possibilities.

Collection of Dukes County Historical Society, Edgartown, Massachusetts.

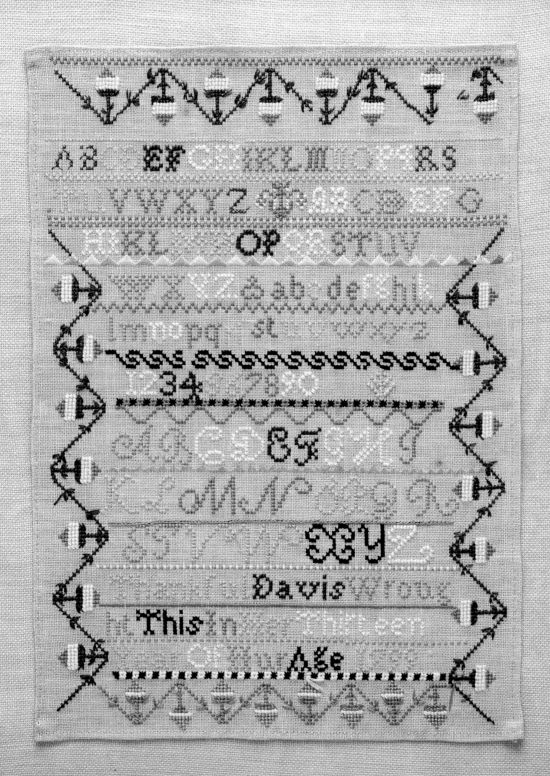

The off-white threads that Thankful used are noticeably thicker than the threads she used for the other colors. They are replicated with four strands of floss.

THANKFUL DAVIS
(11 ½ x 8 ¼ inches, hemmed)

Thankful stitched her sampler on a relatively loosely-woven homespun linen with a count of 35 threads to the inch. The threads she stitched with were tinted with natural dyes locally. Unlike imported silk threads, "dye-pot" threads spun and colored in the home were not uniform in color. Since the thickness of these homespun threads varied, and the amount of time that any given batch steeped in

the dye was not controlled precisely, threads of any one color would often vary in shade and hue.

Thankful worked her sampler from top to bottom, as most American children did, and left her personal trademarks. She referred to herself as both *her* and *hur* and appeared to switch back and forth from single to double thicknesses of thread for no apparent reason.

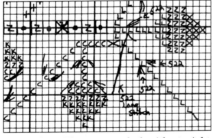

Thankful incorporated multicolored leaves into her borders. They are worked with straight stitches using two strands of floss over two threads. She failed to snip and tuck in a long thread.

Thankful was thirteen when she completed her work. This simple yet whimsical piece was kept in her family until her grandson donated it to the Dukes County Historical Society.

The General Instructions in the Appendix show how to find the starting point and work the stitches.

MATERIALS
17½ x 15¼ inches of 35-count ivory linen, dyed with the #2 Coffee recipe (see Appendix); DMC embroidery floss as shown in the Chart Key (note that the symbols change from one to four strands); size 26 tapestry needle.

Directions
Work this sampler in cross stitch, but note that the number of strands of floss used ranges from one to four, as indicated in the Chart Key.

The original is hemmed, although it is not essential to hem before framing. To replicate the original hems, count four stitches up from the top border. Fold the linen over eight stitches, and repeat for the remaining three sides. Fold again to four stitches on each side in turn, backstitching every other stitch approximately three threads in from the edge of the fabric. Use one strand of lightest green #524.

	CHART KEY	
SYMBOL	DMC #	COLOR
X	420	gold, 2 str.
6 L	936	dk. green: 2 str., 1str.
■	935	darkest green, 2 str.
C	522	lt. green, 2 str.
3	524	lightest green, 4 str.
S	370	olive green, 2 str.
E	926	slate blue, 2 str.
●	310	black, 2 str.
◀	3021	dk. brown, 4 str.
ℓ C	3023	med. gray: 2 str., 4 str.
Y	647	dk. gray, 2 str.
Λ	648	lt. gray, 2 str.
U	841	med. brown, 2 str.
K	612	tan, 2 str.
† 8	613	lt. tan: 2 str., 1 str.
0 Z	822	off-white: 2 str., 4 str.

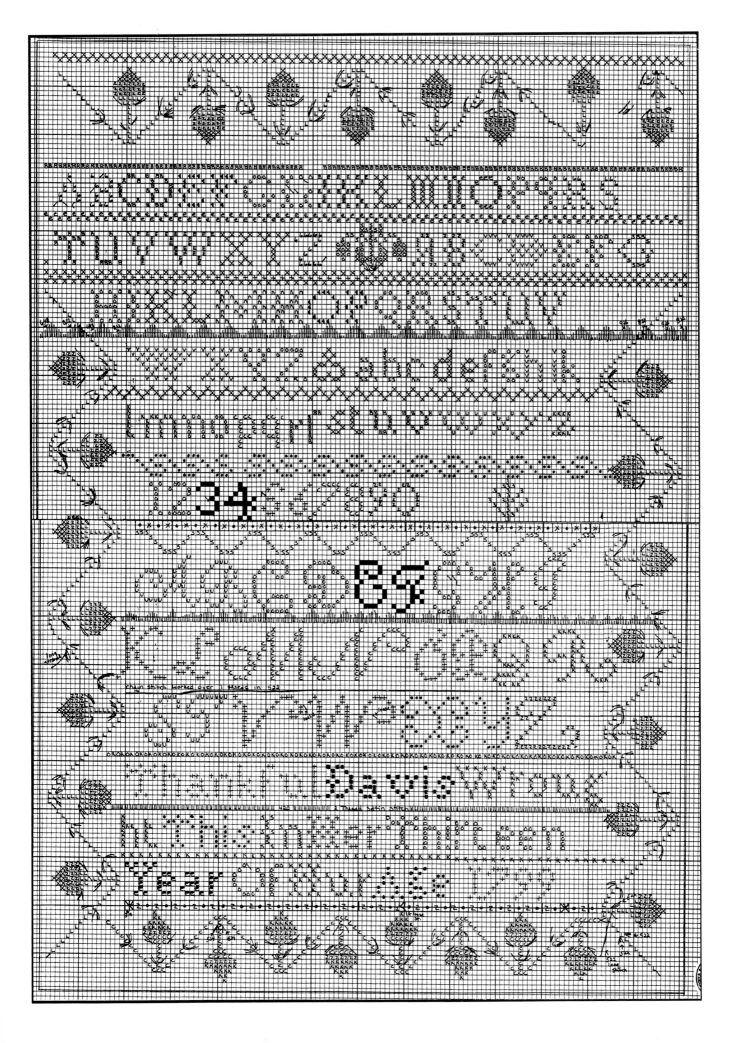

MARTHA & MARY FITZHUGH

A Who's Who of distinguished Virginia families on one square of linen.

Martha "Patsy" Fitzhugh was seven years old when she began to chronicle the family genealogy including the death dates of her older sisters, Lucy and Betty. She left it unfinished when she died in 1793, ironically after having stitched the word "Hence" in the verse. Her sister, Mary Lee "Molly" Fitzhugh, probably finished it.

Mary Fitzhugh married George Washington Parke Custis, who was the grandson of Martha Washington from her first marriage to Daniel Custis. Later, Martha's second husband, George Washington, adopted her grandson. Mary Fitzhugh's own daughter, Mary Anna, married Robert E. Lee and brought the sampler with her to the Custis-Lee Mansion (now Arlington House). It was left behind when they moved south at the start of the Civil War following Lee's appointment as General of the Northern Virginia army.

Collection of Arlington House, R. E. Lee Memorial, Arlington, Virginia.

William Fitzhugh born September 4th 1741 ✦✦ Ann Randolph born
May 13th 1747 ✦✦ They were married April 2d 1763 ✦✦ Lucy Fitz—
hugh born November 2d 1771 died September 29th 1777 ✦✦ Betty
Randolph Fitzhugh born November 20th 1773 died October 10th 1774

Here Innocence and Beauty lie, whose Breath

Was snatch'd by early, not untimely Death.

Hence did they go just as they did begin

Sorrow to Know, before they knew to Sin.

Death, that does Sin and Sorrow thus prevent,

Is the next Blessing to a Life well spent.

✦✦ Randolph Fitzhugh ✦✦ ... ... Martha Cart...
born February 28th ... ... September 29th ... died my this
ampler ... ... the Word Hence, which was the ... ...
... prophet ... ... Lawrence Death ✦✦ ... ...

Her Name shall liv... ... ...
And (this in Dust) her Memory shall bloom.
Tho' I deplore my Loss and wish it less,
Yet will I kiss the Rod and acquiesce.

Mary Lee Fitzhugh born April 22nd 1758 ✦✦✦✦✦✦✦✦✦
William Henry Fitzhugh born March 9th 1792 ✦✦✦✦✦✦✦✦

MARTHA & MARY FITZHUGH

(18½ x 17 inches)

Interspersed with somber poetic passages, this sampler chronicles the births, marriages, and deaths of the Fitzhugh family. Martha "Patsy" Fitzhugh began the work, but left it unfinished when she died at the age of seven. Prophetically, the last word she stitched was *Hence*. One or both of her sisters, Mary and Ann, are thought to have finished it. Perhaps it was Patsy's early death that dictated the use of so much black thread. That and the verses give the funereal cast of a mourning sampler to Martha's piece, which was originally intended to record the family tree.

Some of the stitching in the original sampler, shown in the photo on the preceding page, has disintegrated so badly it cannot be read. That portion of the sampler appears at the bottom of this page and the full text has been reproduced in the caption.

The General Instructions in the Appendix show how to find the starting point and work the stitches.

MATERIALS

24½ x 23 inches of 35-count ivory linen, dyed with the #3 & #4 Coffee recipes (see Appendix); DMC embroidery floss as shown in the Chart Key (note any variations in number of strands); size 26 tapestry needle.

DIRECTIONS

The original linen measures 18½ by 17 inches (35-x 32-count). To make yours as square as the original, remove three horizontal threads per inch for 19 inches. Work the border in eyelet stitch. Cross stitch the letters, using half-, quarter-, or three-quarter stitches, to simulate disintegration.

A Genealogical Journey from Custis to Washington to Lewis to Fitzhugh to Lee

It starts with John Parke Custis, an English sea captain who settled in the American colony of Virginia. On the Eastern Shore he built a house which he called Arlington. One of John's sons, Daniel, married Martha Dandridge and they had two children, one of whom was also named John Parke Custis. When Daniel died, his wife Martha married General George Washington and moved with her children into Mount Vernon. Young John (who married Lord Baltimore's niece) did not fight in the Revolutionary War but asked his stepfather to let him come to Yorktown to view the battlefield. There he caught camp fever, and, at his deathbed, General Washington agreed to adopt his stepson John's two youngest children,

Eleanor Custis and George Washington Parke Custis. When Eleanor married Lawrence Lewis, George and Martha Washington gave them a beautiful brick plantation home three miles from Mount Vernon, called Woodlawn. (Lawrence Lewis was the uncle of Betty Washington Lewis, whose sampler is also included in this collection.) George Washington Parke Custis built a grand home, Arlington House, where Robert E. Lee came to court his daughter. George did not approve. However, his wife, Mary Lee Fitzhugh Custis (who worked on this sampler), and his sister, Eleanor Parke Custis, pled Lee's case successfully, whereupon Mary Anna Custis married Robert E. Lee.

	CHART KEY	
SYMBOL	**DMC #**	**COLOR**
O •	310	black: 1 str., 2 str.
■		3 str.
+	3371	darkest brown-black
Z	830	gold

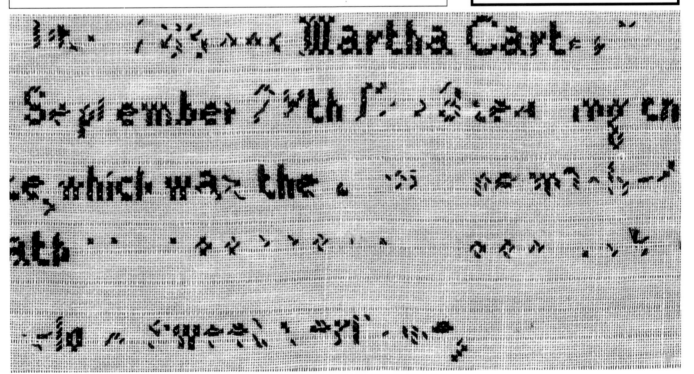

The disintegrated stitching shown in the photo of the original sampler on the preceding page originally read: **Ann Randolph Fitzhugh born June 30th, 1783 Martha Carter Fitzhugh born February 28th 1786 died September 29th 1793 leaving this sampler unfinished, the Word Hence, which was the last she marked being prophetic of her lamented Death.**

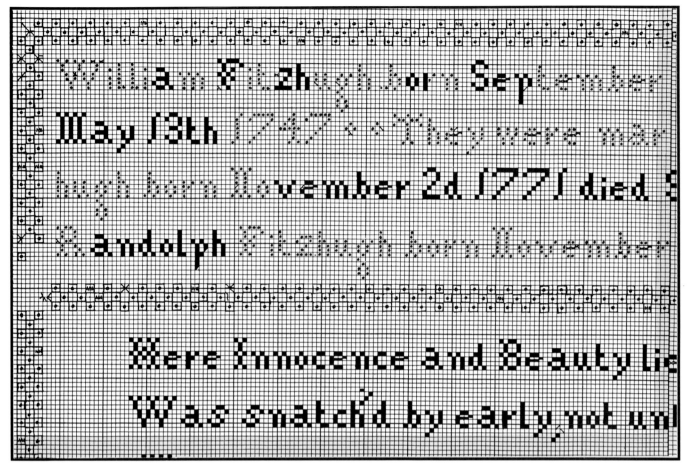

Shaded portions of charts indicate overlap with sections on this and following pages.

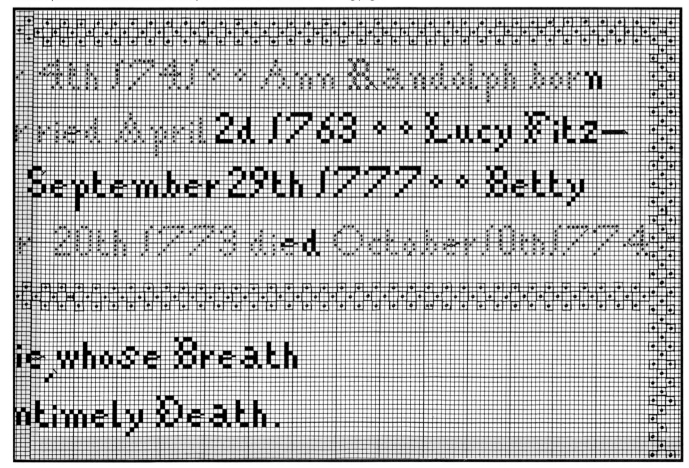

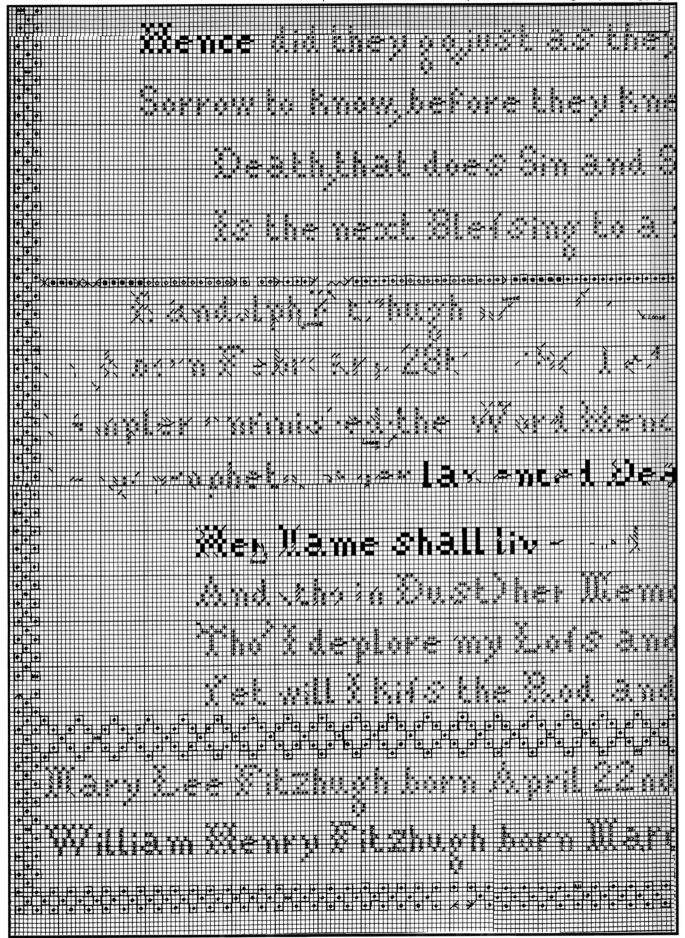

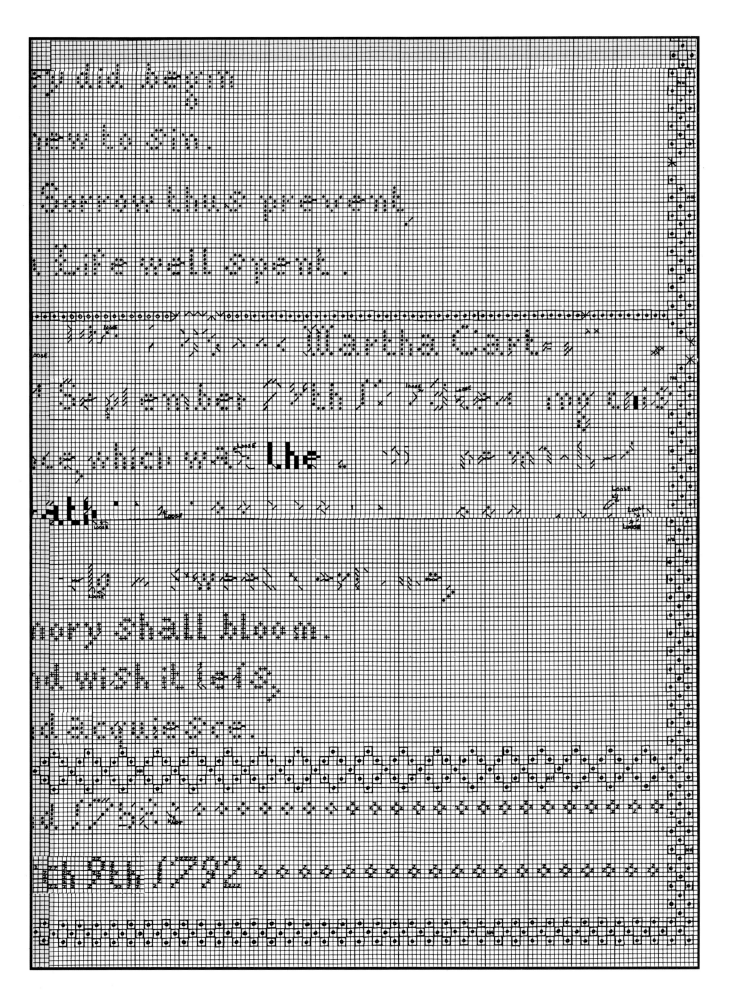

SOPHIA WATERS

An independent spirit from Bennington who cared not for precision.

Sophia was born in Bennington, Vermont, on December 2, 1793, to Captain Oliver and Phoebe Beebe Waters. She finished her sampler when she was ten years old, probably working under her mother's direction. Sophia was a confident and lively girl who enjoyed many friendships before leaving home at the age of eighteen to earn her living. She worked at a variety of jobs, including a stint as a "spinster" in a woolen factory. (The word "spinster" originally referred to a person who spun wool, but since this was a common way for an unmarried woman to support herself, the term eventually developed the connotation it has today.) As you might have guessed from the no-nonsense style of her work, stitching this sampler was not the high point of Sophia's life.

A B C D E F G
H I J K L M N O
P Q R S T U V W
W X Y Z &.

a b c d e f g h i j k l
m n o p q r s t u v
w x y z

1 2 3 4 5 6 7 8 9 10 11

Sophia Waters
Bennington
August the 8 1803
Mark'd in the 10 year
of her age

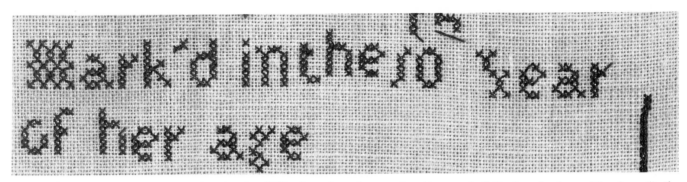

Sophia's use of the word "marked," (condensed to "mark'd") reflects the original function a sampler was intended to perform, that of a record of letter-forms and number-forms used to identify household linens—hence the name "marking sampler." The formal cadence of the phrase "in the 10th year of her age," can also be found on tombstones of the period. She inserted a crown, a printer's symbol, at the end of her uppercase alphabet.

SOPHIA WATERS
(11 ½ x 5 ¾ inches)

The charm of this sampler is in its straightforward, unadorned effort to participate in a tradition. In that sense it is like the work of an untrained, folk painter. The obvious facts that she rarely executed a perfect stitch and that her borders are not straight seem unimportant beside the poignant sense of honest effort her piece conveys. Apparently she had as little access to a range of colors as she did to formal training. The spare, monochromatic ground, however, makes the few spots of bright blue seem more precious.

Disintegration accounts for some of the hanging threads, but many are due to her failure to tuck them in.

The General Instructions in the Appendix show how to find the starting point and work the stitches

MATERIALS
16½ x 11¾ inches of 35-count ivory linen, dyed with the #3 Coffee recipe (see Appendix); DMC embroidery floss as shown in the Chart Key (note the variations in number of strands); size 26 tapestry needle.

DIRECTIONS
Though some of Sophia's stitches appear to be half stitches because they are worked out of line a half-thread up, they are only displaced stitches worked as full cross stitches. Although it is not current practice to allow loose threads to hang on the front, as she did, to do so will make the finished piece an authentic copy.

C H A R T	K E Y	
SYMBOL	**DMC #**	**COLOR**
✳ ☒	3371	darkest black-brown: 4 str., 2 str.
◖ ●	3021	brown: 2 str., 4 str.
⋀	924	teal blue

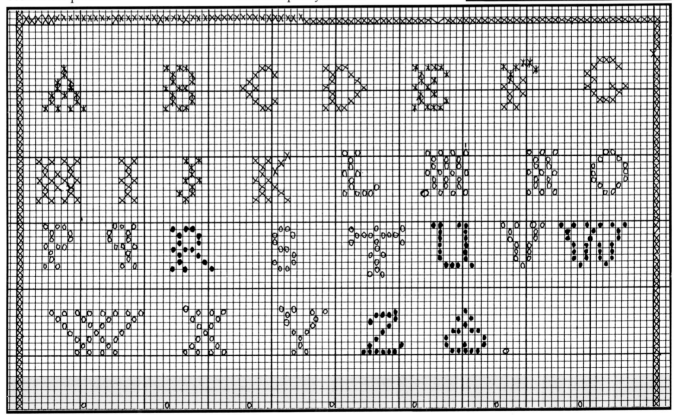

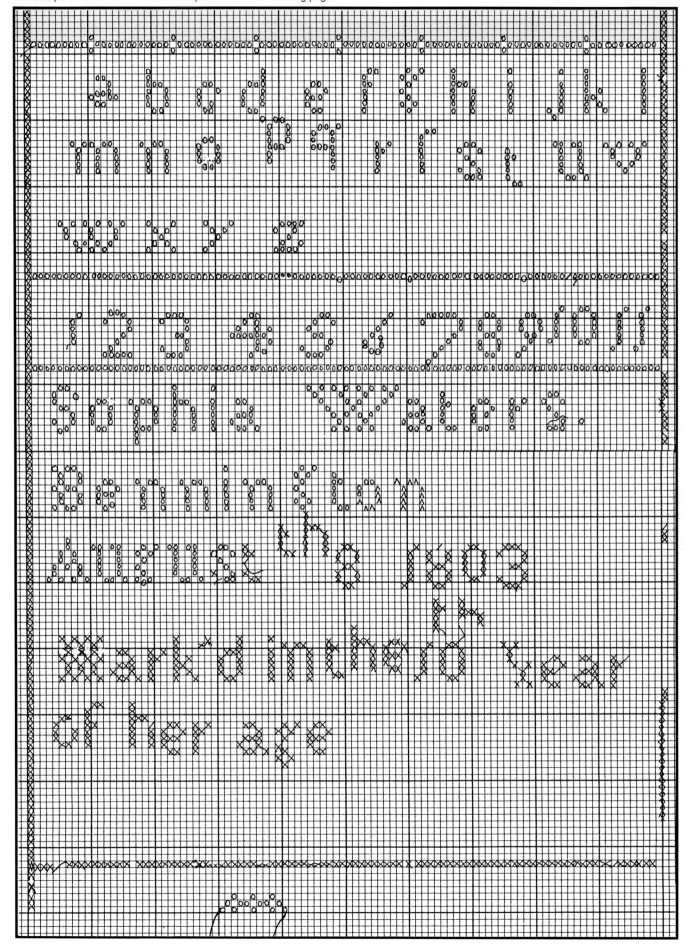

CHARLOTTE FROBISHER

A gorgeous array of borders, stars, flowers, and "Honor thy mother."

When Charlotte stitched her sampler in 1805, President Thomas Jefferson was in the middle of his first term in office. Though she was only nine years old, this unusually sophisticated piece could not have been her first sampler. Beyond this work no tangible record remains of her life.

Hers is an excellent example of the Federal-style sampler with floral motifs in ornate urns and elaborate vertical borders. The colors she chose for those borders are an arresting combination—a beautiful aqua-blue with what were once two shades of rose-colored flowers, now faded to light brown. The vivid blue that remains can only be reproduced with silk thread. She worked the flowers in the top border in shades of lavender seldom seen in New England samplers. For some reason the reds in the bottom border have remained unusually bright over the years.

Collection of Essex Institute, Salem, Massachusetts.

ABCDEFGHIJI
KLMNOPQRSS
TUVWXYZ&

abcdefghiklmnopqrstuvwxyz

Honor thy mother
for her arms
Secur'd thee from
A thousand harms

Charlotte Frobisher,
aged 9 1805.

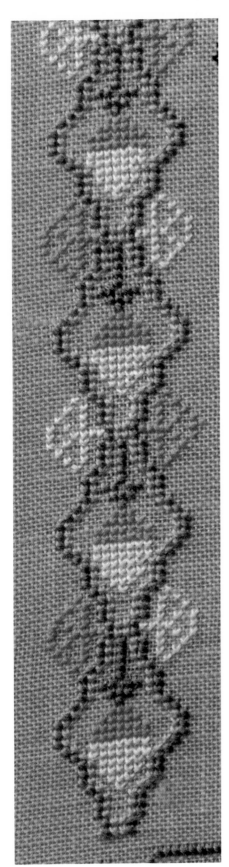

CHARLOTTE FROBISHER

(16½ x 11¾ inches)

Though little is known about Charlotte's background, the variety of her colors and designs, some quite exotic, are clues that she came from a prosperous, perhaps culturally rich, family. The side borders, for example, appear to have been inspired by Asian-Indian designs, suggesting exposure to imported fabrics or furnishings. She also had access to many bright colors. At the time Charlotte stitched this, most of the silk thread dyed in bright colors had to be imported. Her bright red thread was certainly imported, possibly a gift brought back from international travels. The top and bottom borders both use the traditional strawberry design but in very different color schemes.

The General Instructions in the Appendix show how to find the starting point and work the stitches.

MATERIALS

22½ x 17¾ inches of 25-count mocha linen, dyed with the #2 Coffee recipe (see Appendix); DMC embroidery floss or Au Ver a Soie® silk as shown in the Chart Key (note that the original was stitched entirely in silk—this reproduction uses silk only in the blue and the yellow-green of the side borders); size 24 tapestry needle.

Though the overall look of this sampler is ornate, the two stars, which quilters call "simple" or "variable" stars, are reminiscent of simple country piecework. Like many traditional folk designs, however, motifs like this are also found in ancient Asian cultures.

DIRECTIONS

Work this sampler entirely in cross stitch. The borders are worked in silk because it offers a superior color match. Use only one strand of silk but two of floss unless noted otherwise.

Some stitches are missing, either due to disintegration or because Charlotte forgot to cross them. In three places she was forced to remove stitches to get out of trouble, but she snipped the linen by accident and had to mend it. The chart marks those mends with numbers and shows how you can replicate them without your having actually to cut your own linen.

 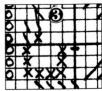

Charlotte was not shy about exposing her mistakes. When she accidentally clipped threads she sometimes mended them with different colors, such as this bright yellow one.

CHART KEY		
SYMBOL	DMC/Au Ver a Soie®	COLOR
◤	131	blue: silk, 1 str.
=	2223	gold: silk, 1 str.
I	676	lt. gold
Z	928	lightest slate blue
E	3041	lt. lavender
K	350	red
V	945	peach
H	734	olive green
8	543	off-white
✗	744	yellow: mending sts.
A	435	lt. brown
■	3047	lt. yellow
+	504	lightest blue-green
M	503	lt. blue-green: 4 mending sts.
• ❘	502	med. blue-green: 1 str., 4 str.
O Ø	407	old rose: 1 str., 3 str.
– ■	869	brown: 1 str., 2 str.
❘	3021	dk. brown: 1 str., for verse, name & date
❘ X ✳	310	black: 1 str.for lowercase alphabet, 2 str., 1 str.
>		white

Note that each of the enclosed flowers in the side borders varies slightly. They progress from a dark brown at the bottom to lighter browns at the top. This grounds the design while giving these ornate figures the effect of an almost spiritual lightness.

MARY LEE

An historic southern family whose plantation home survives to this day.

Though much older than he, Mary was first cousin to Robert E. Lee, a leader of the Confederacy during the Civil War. Her mother's maiden name was Armistead. Her father, Thomas Lee, was known as Ludwell, which is how Mary referred to him where she stitched her parents' names and date of marriage. If you look closely in the lower left corner, you will see the name of her family plantation. Belmont's main house, privately owned, still stands.

Mary's father helped Thomas Jefferson write the Religious Freedoms Act of 1777 for Virginia. Mary's parents felt strongly that an end to slavery had to be found, and her father's family introduced legislation to that effect in Virginia. In fact, the family freed the slaves of Belmont Plantation in 1791, eight years before the slaves at Mount Vernon were freed upon George Washington's death. Ironically, however, Mary became mistress of a slave plantation in South Carolina after she married.

Collection of Arlington House, R. E. Lee Memorial, Arlington, Virginia.

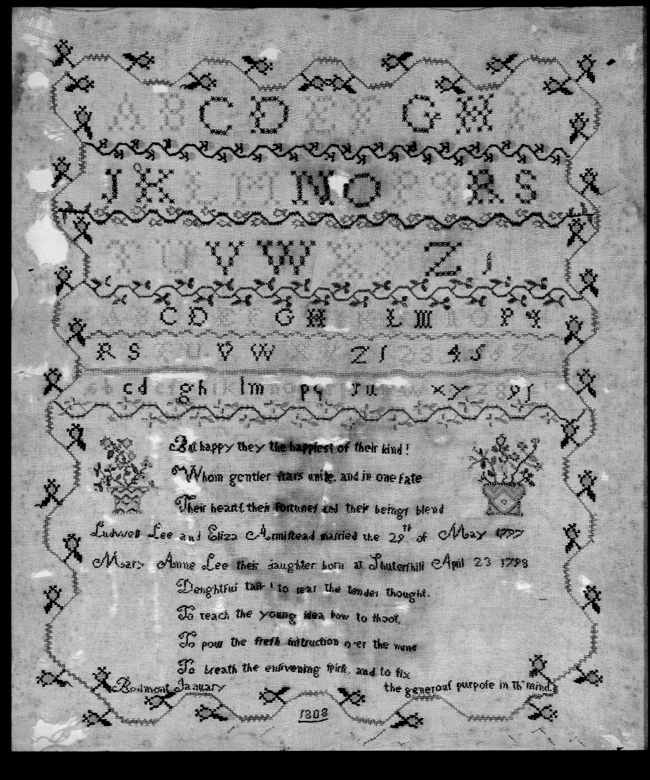

A B C D E F G H I

J K L M N O P Q R S

T U V W X Y Z

A B C D E F G H I K L M N O P Q

R S T U V W X Y Z 1 2 3 4 5 6 7

a b c d e f g h i k l m n o p q r s t u v w x y z & 1

But happy they the happiest of their kind!

Whom gentler stars unite, and in one fate

Their hearts their fortunes and their beings blend

Ludwell Lee and Eliza Armistead married the 29th of May 1777

Mary Anne Lee their daughter born at Shuterhill April 23 1798

Delightful task! to rear the tender thought,

To teach the young idea how to shoot,

To pour the fresh instruction o'er the mind

To breath the enlivening spirit, and to fix

Belmont January   the generous purpose in th'mind.

1303

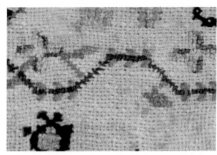

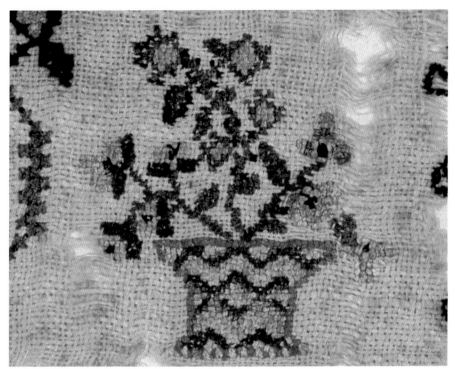

In the floral motif on the left side of her sampler Mary created a basket which suggests the woven basket designs done by native Americans. It is quite possible that she had seen such a basket herself.

Mary must have been fond of roses. She lavished attention to the rosebuds in her dividing bands by stitching them all over one thread.

The roses in the border are unusual because they are stitched over both one and two threads. Belmont was the name of the plantation on which Mary lived.

MARY LEE
(17½ x 14¼ inches)

Mary's sampler stands today as a testament to unusual patience. Stitching over only one thread is tedious to begin with, but working so many over-ones on unevenweave fabric must have demanded extraordinary concentration and untiring eyesight. She used the printer's *S* throughout her sampler.

The General Instructions in the Appendix show how to convert evenweave to unevenweave linen, find the starting point and work the stitches.

MATERIALS
23½ x 20 inches of 32-count cream linen, dyed with the #1 Coffee recipe (see Appendix); DMC embroidery floss as shown in the Chart Key (see footnotes for variations in number of strands and over-ones); size 26 tapestry needle.

DIRECTIONS
Mary used unevenweave linen that measured 34- by 30-count. To recreate that from 34-count evenweave, locate a point three inches down from the top and in from each side border. Moving straight down the center of the fabric, slide a needle under every fifteenth thread and snip it. Pull each snipped piece from the center toward the edge of the fabric. Anchor the snipped end of each thread about an inch from the edge, using hand or machine stitches. (See the Appendix for a more detailed description.)

Work the entire piece with two strands of floss, including stitches worked over one thread. All of the over-ones are graphed with this symbol ▮ regardless of color. You will find it easier to work from the chart, especially the baskets, if you have the chart enlarged to 200% of its present size. All of the verse is stitched over one thread.

The chart provides additional information by inserting footnote numbers here and there. This is what those numbers mean:

1: When you work the rosebuds in the border, stitch the outside color green, #500, over two threads, but stitch the inside color rose, #407, over one thread.

2: Work the verse in black, #310, with two strands of floss but over one thread.

3: Work all the rosebuds in all three of the horizontal dividing bands over one thread.

4: Work the baskets on both sides over one thread.

5: Work the little blue flowers in the dividing band that has the darker blue veins all over one thread.

6: When you work the first and third horizontal bands, use #500 for the stem and leaves; use #407 for the buds; use #500 for the second stem; use #502 green around the bud.

CHART KEY		
SYMBOL	**DMC #**	**COLOR**
U	3041	lavender
V	500	darkest blue-green
✳	502	med. blue-green
X ▮	310	black, over-ones
•	407	lt. rose
◤	524	lightest green
K	830	dk. green-gold
3	833	lt. green-gold
Z	931	blue
O	927	lt. slate blue
▪	676	gold
E	3042	lt. lavender

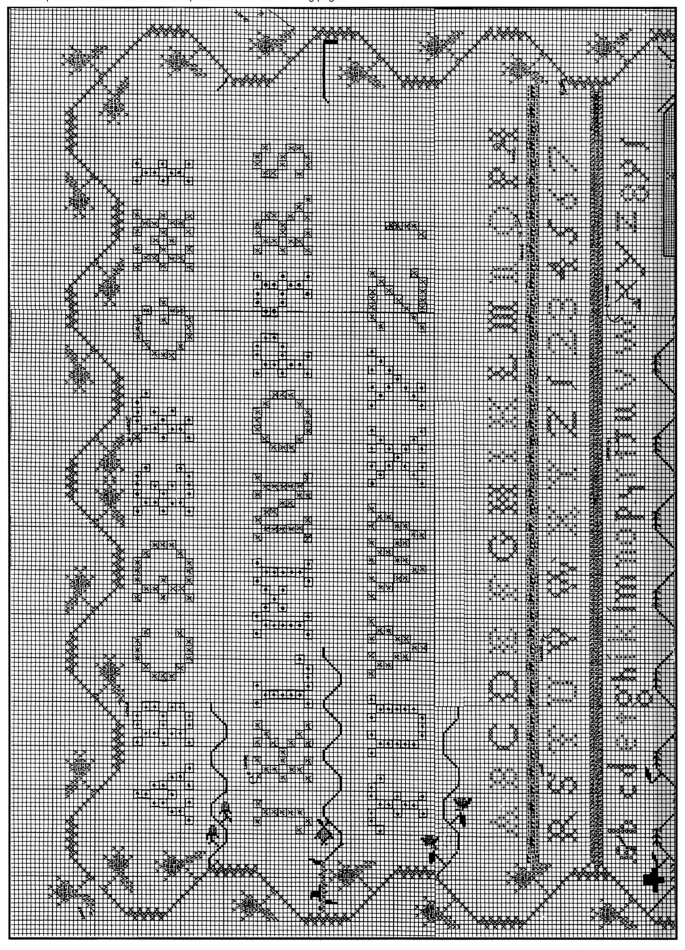

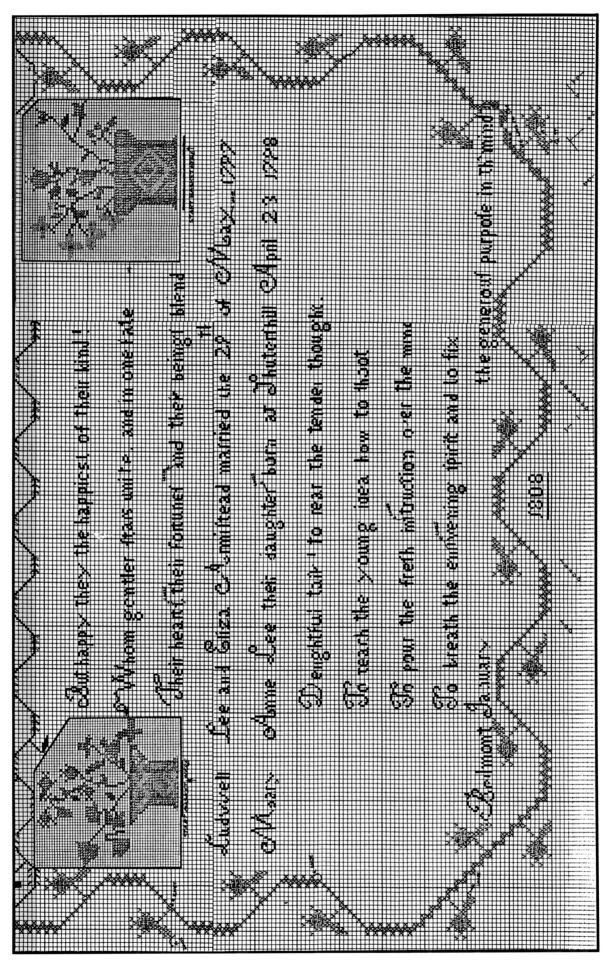

So happy they the happiest of their kind!
When gentler stars unite, and in one fate

Their hearts, their fortunes and their beings blend

Ludwell Lee and Eliza Armistead married the 2⁰ of May 1797

Mars Anne Lee their daughter born at Shuterhill April 23 1778

Delightful task! to rear the tender thought.

To teach the young idea how to shoot

To pour the fresh instruction o'er the mind

To breath the enlivening spirit and to fix

the generous purpose in the mind

Belmont January 1808

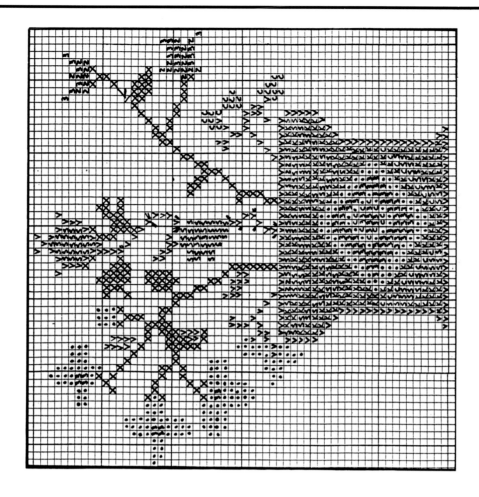

BETTY WASHINGTON LEWIS

George Washington's great-niece, named for his only sister.

Betty was born in Richmond, Virginia, on October 14, 1796, and was the namesake for her paternal grand-mother—George Washington's only sister. The first Betty Washington married Colonel Fielding Lewis and became the mistress of Kenmore, their estate in Fredericksburg, Virginia. The land surrounding that lovely brick home was the site of historic battles during both the Revolutionary and Civil wars. Surprisingly, the house still stands.

Since her parents were prosperous, Betty had access to a large canvas and rich-colored threads in red, blue, and green. As many girls did, she selected a passage that praises virtue and denounces vice. This message, and her desire to please her parents, may have inspired her to stitch such an unusually lovely sampler. Hers was not rolled up and stored like most, but framed in silver leaf.

Collection of Kenmore Association, Fredericksburg, Virginia.

ABCDEFGHIJKLMNO

PQRSTUVWXYZ

ABCDEFGHIJKLMNOPQRSTUVWX

YZ . 1234567891011121314151617 1819

Learn to contemn all Praise betimes
For Flattery is the Nurse of Crimes
With early Virtue plant thy Breast
The specious Arts of Vice detest

take

Youth like softened Wax with Ease will
Those Images that first Impressions make
If those be fair their Actions will be bright
If foul they'll clouded be with Shades of
Night

Betty Washington Lewis February 25th
1805

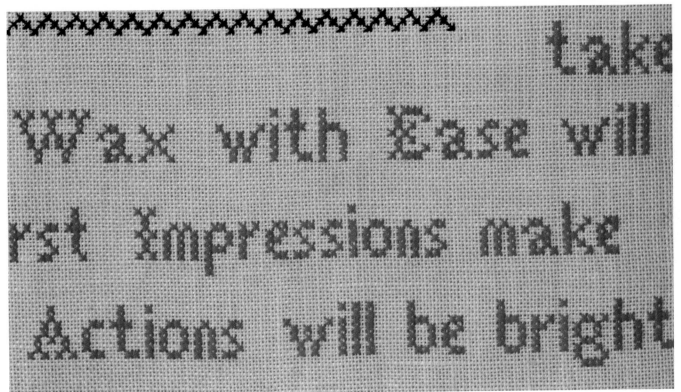

It is not at all uncommon to see the final word, or even a few letters placed above or below a line that has run out of room. A rhyming verse is unforgiving in this respect because, unlike a decorative border, or even a name and date, transposing or deleting words in a rhyme can ruin the effect of a verse. Betty was forced to place the word **take** above the line, as shown, and work **night** below the last line of the same verse. At the time this was stitched, writers were free to capitalize words as they chose to lend them emphasis in the context of the sentence.

BETTY WASHINGTON LEWIS
(20 x 15 ¼ inches)

Betty was eight years old when she finished this piece. Her materials indicate that her family was relatively prosperous. She had available to her silk embroidery threads in a palette of unusual colors. Unfortunately, exposure to light has caused the colors of the stitches in the original to fade so badly that the Kenmore Association, in whose care it is, requested that the colors of the original threads be approximated in this reproduction.

Like many stitchers of schoolgirl samplers in her day, Betty selected verses that praise virtue and caution the young to beware temptation. The educational value of these moral strictures is probably the reason why this sampler was framed. Most samplers were rolled up and stored in drawers, but the sampler on display at Kenmore is encased in a silver-leaf frame that is as old as the sampler itself, so it is likely to be the original frame.

 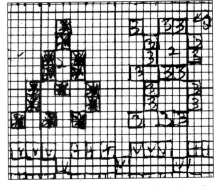

Betty used eyelet stitches in varying thicknesses for her top alphabet as well as alternating colors for each letter. However, notice that in the first dividing band she incorporated two colors instead of one.

The General Instructions in the Appendix show how to find the starting point and work the stitches.

MATERIALS
26 x 21¼ inches of 25-count mocha linen, dyed with the #1 Coffee recipe (see Appendix); DMC embroidery floss as shown in the Chart Key (note any variations in number of strands); size 24 tapestry needle.

DIRECTIONS
When working this sampler, pay close attention to variations in thread color. Work entirely in cross stitch, except for the top alphabet which is worked in the eyelet stitch.

CHART KEY		
SYMBOL	DMC #	COLOR
●	500	dk. blue-green, 1 str.
Ꮾ ③	3371	darkest brown-black: 1 str., 2 str.
✳ ✗	347	red: 1 str., 2 str.
✛	311	navy
Ⴘ	561	bright green
▣	502	med. blue-green

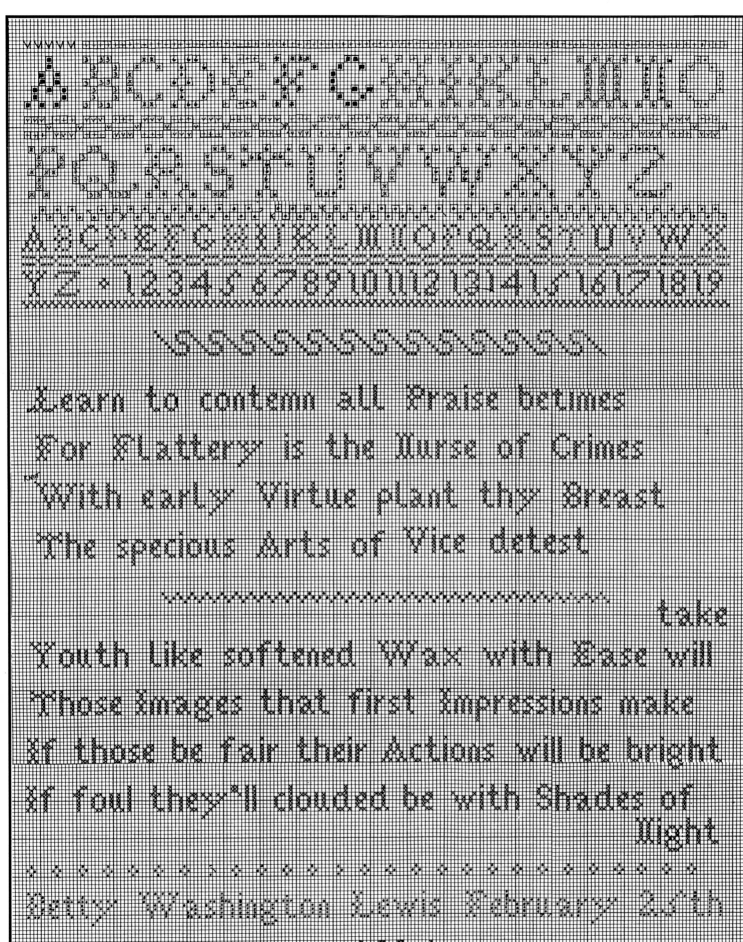

ABCDEFGHIKLMNO
PQRSTUVWXYZ

ABCDEFGHIKLMNOPQRSTUVWX
YZ 1234567891011121314151617181910

Learn to contemn all Praise betimes
For Flattery is the Nurse of Crimes
With early Virtue plant thy Breast
The specious Arts of Vice detest

take

Youth Like softened Wax with Ease will
Those Images that first Impressions make
If those be fair their Actions will be bright
If foul they'll clouded be with Shades of
Night

Betty Washington Lewis February 20th

1801

MARY ROBINSON

She displayed her command of stitchery in a schoolgirl masterpiece.

 Mary's sampler was not the only place "crowded with sins" in 1814. Three months after this ten-year-old child completed her versatile stitching in Exeter, New Hampshire, the British invaded Maryland and burned the Capitol and the White House.

The verse in this sampler was part of a repertoire taught in schools, so hers is likely to be a schoolgirl sampler. Her planning was good but not perfect. The last line of the verse went a bit long, and she had to drop the letter *J* from her lowercase alphabet and the *I* from her cursive letters.

The four-sided stitch makes the initial capitals of her name and age more emphatic. Notice the birds on either side of the last line. Did she finish her work in May, when the robins return to New England? Or are these flanking symbols for her family name?

Collection of Museum of Fine Arts, Boston, Massachusetts.

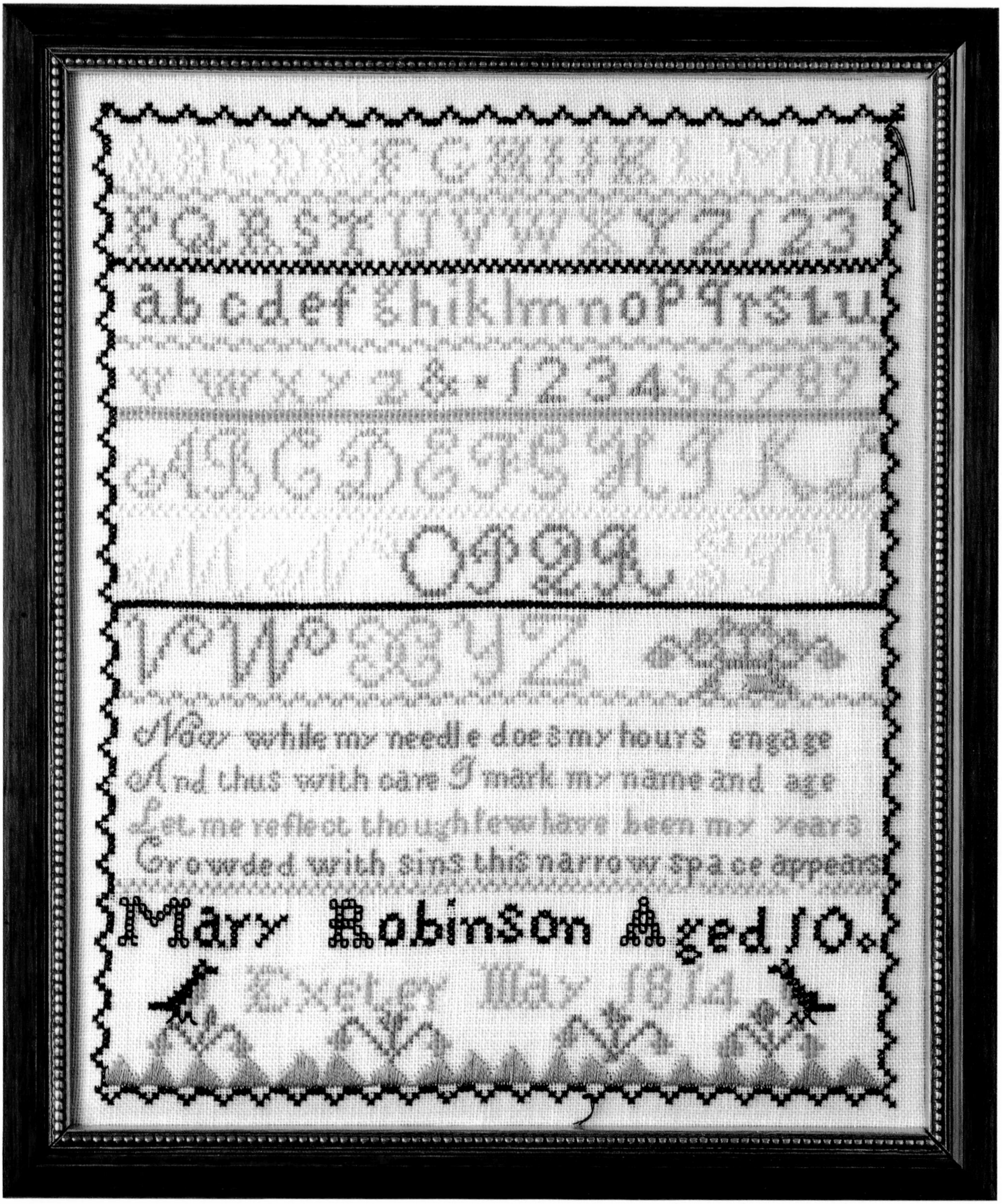

ABCDEFGHIJKLMNO

PQRSTUVWXYZ123

ab c d e f ghiklmno Pqrstu

v wx y z & 123456789

ABCDEFGHIJKL

MNO OPQR STU

V W XYZ

Now while my needle does my hours engage
And thus with care I mark my name and age
Let me reflect thought few have been my years
Crowded with sins this narrow space appears

Mary Robinson Aged 10.

Exeter May 1814

 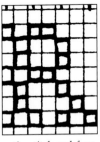

Mary mastered both the satin stitch and four-sided stitch. She used the challenging four-sided stitch only in the first letters of her name and age. One wonders if she meant to draw attention to them or tired of the stitch, so used it sparingly.

MATERIALS

16¼ x 14¾ inches of 30-count ivory linen dyed with the #1 Tea recipe (see Appendix); DMC embroidery floss as shown in the Chart Key (note that #648 is stitched over one thread); size 24 tapestry needle.

DIRECTIONS

If you choose to hemstitch around the edge of the sampler, use #734 thread. Work the hemstitch nine inches from the edge of the border on all four sides; the turnover edge is three stitches. Alternatively, you may backstitch in #734 along the border to simulate the hemstitching.

When working this sampler refer to the following footnotes with the corresponding numbers on the chart:

1: First line of verse, #502.
2: Second line of verse, #648.
3: Third line of verse, #407.
4: Fourth line of verse, #502.
5: Backstitch bird's claw in #310.
6: Small knot with one-inch tail.

It is difficult to tell whether young children copied objects like the birds in Mary's sampler from their own observations of nature or from books. Even though she chose black thread instead of brown for the back feathers of her robins, one can assume that a New England child named Robinson would have had one pointed out to her by the time she was nine years old.

MARY ROBINSON

(10 ¼ x 8 ¾ inches)

This charming sampler was probably stitched while Mary was attending a school. Her school training shows in her use of the four-sided stitch in the first letters of her name and in the satin-stitched sawtooth border across the bottom.

The stitch left hanging in the top border could have been caused by disintegration, or she simply neglected to tuck it in. The waste knot at the bottom was never buried properly.

The background in the original sampler remains ivory. Though it has shaded slightly gray with age, this only enhances the colors Mary chose to work with—rose, blue-green, gold, pewter grey, slate blue, and, a pink, now faded into the background.

The General Instructions in the Appendix show how to find the starting point and work the stitches.

CHART KEY		
SYMBOL	DMC #	COLOR
✖	310	black
◣	822	off-white
•	647	lt. gray
✚	927	lt. slate blue
▢	734	olive green
− ▮	502	med. blue green, 1 str
V ▮	407	lt. rose, 1 str.
▮	648	med. gray, over-one stitch

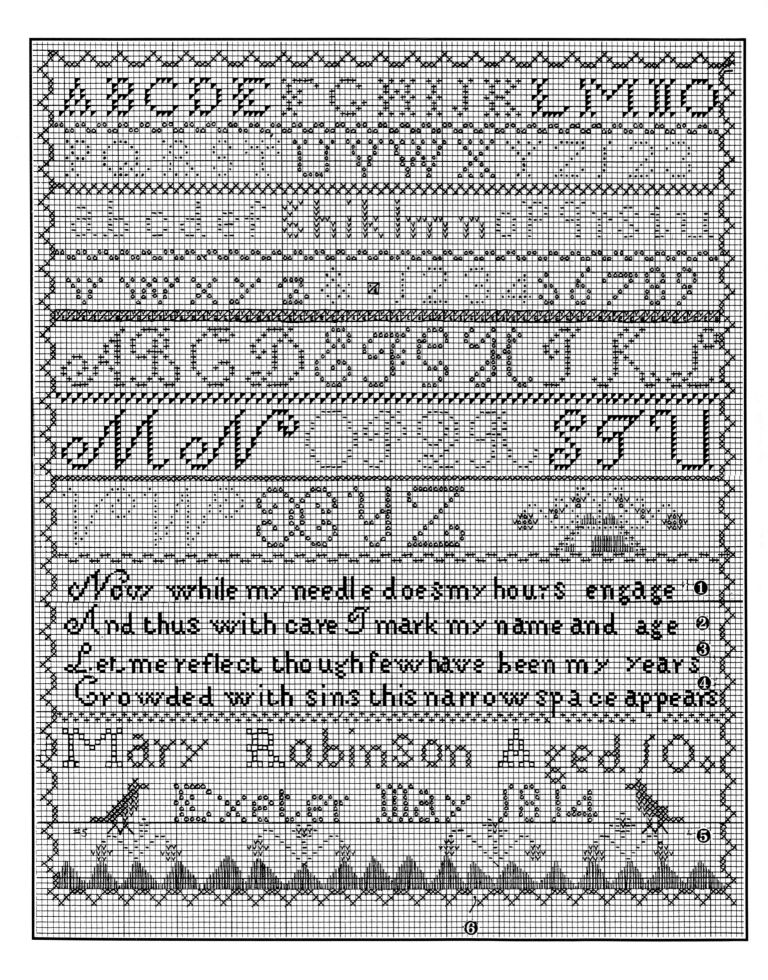

ELIZA HALL

Though only seven years old, she ranks among the best stitchers of all.

 Eliza Hall was born on April 30, 1810, in Boston, Massachusetts. She married David Hough Ela in January of 1832 at the age of twenty-two. She died on a Monday in November of 1837 at the age of twenty-seven.

She learned to stitch at a school where it is very likely she produced a simpler marking sampler before she stitched this one. This sampler, which probably took over a year to complete, contains some of the most skillful stitching in this collection. Never once did Eliza stitch over an incorrect number of threads, even when she was working over one thread. Furthermore, her ground is a slippery unevenweave linen on which cross stitches tend to slide from a half-cross into a straight line. It would be quite an accomplishment for an adult to have produced such a work. For a seven-year-old, it is truly an amazing feat.

Collection of Museum of Fine Arts, Boston, Massachusetts.

Happy the woman who can find
Constant employment in her mind
She for amusement need not roam
Her pleasure centre in her home

Eliza Hall, Aged 7,
October 8, 1817

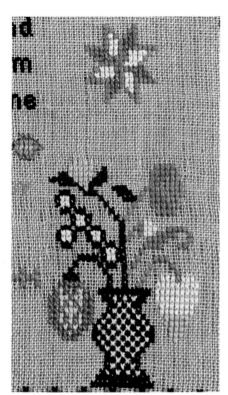

Eliza coordinated the colors in her border with the two identical vases at the bottom of her piece, one worked in blues, and one in rose or brown. Her star looks almost like piecework.

ELIZA HALL
(12⅛ x 12 inches)

Eliza stitched her sampler on unevenweave linen that measured 13 inches high (29 threads per inch) by 11 inches wide (32 threads per inch). If worked on evenweave linen, the piece will come out virtually square, as the stitch count is 181 stitches high by 187 stitches wide. Unevenweave fabrics available today, like the one used to stitch the sampler on the preceding page, are slightly darker than the piece on which Eliza worked her original.

The General Instructions in the Appendix show how to replicate unevenweave linen, find the starting point, and work the stitches.

MATERIALS
18⅜ x 17½ inches of unevenweave linen, dyed a very light brown using the #1 Tea recipe (see Appendix); DMC embroidery floss in colors as indicated in the Chart Key (note where one strand each of two different colors is blended); size 26 tapestry needle.

DIRECTIONS
Eliza stitched her entire piece in cross stitch. Except for the alphabet and verse, which are stitched over only one thread, all stitches are done over two threads. Refer to the footnote numbers on the chart as follows:

1 and 2: Stitch the lowercase alphabet and the *Happy the woman...* verse over only one thread in #310.

3: Stitch the motto *Remember now...* over only one thread in #407.

4: Stitch Eliza's name, age, and the date over only one thread in #823.

Unfortunately, much of the stitching in the dark-colored over-ones has disintegrated somewhat. For example, the brown may have been a bright rose, and the beige a true pink when she first stitched it in 1817. However, most of the lovely original colors, especially the blues, remain vibrant to this day.

Eliza chose a traditional "strawberry" border.

CHART KEY		
SYMBOL	**DMC #**	**COLOR**
☒	935	dk. green
☐	733	lt. green
◵	931	blue
◤	739	lt. cream
Z	950	flesh
L	747	lt. blue
W	543	off-white
■ c +	407	lt. rose: 1 str., 2 str., 2 str.
●	869/3064	brown/rose: 1 str. ea.
3	642/644	beige/lt. beige: 1 str. ea.
T	3046	lt. yellow
–	422	lt. brown
+	436	med. brown
■	310	black
■ ○	823	navy: 1 str., 2 str.

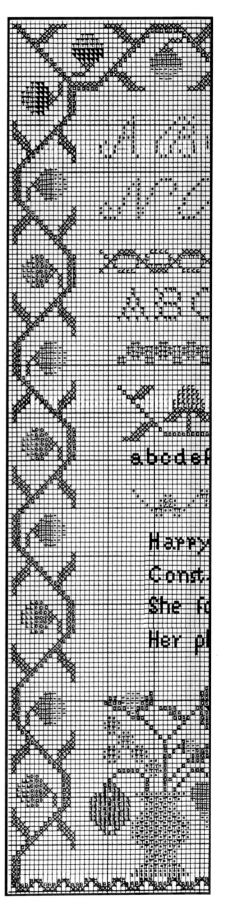

Shaded portions of chart indicate overlap with sections on facing pages.

efghijklmnopqrstuvwxyz 1234 56789
1
ey the woman who can find
stant employment in her mind
for amusement need not roam
pleasure centre in her home
2
Remember now thy Creator
in the days of thy youth
3
Eliza Hall, Aged 7,
4
October 8, 1817

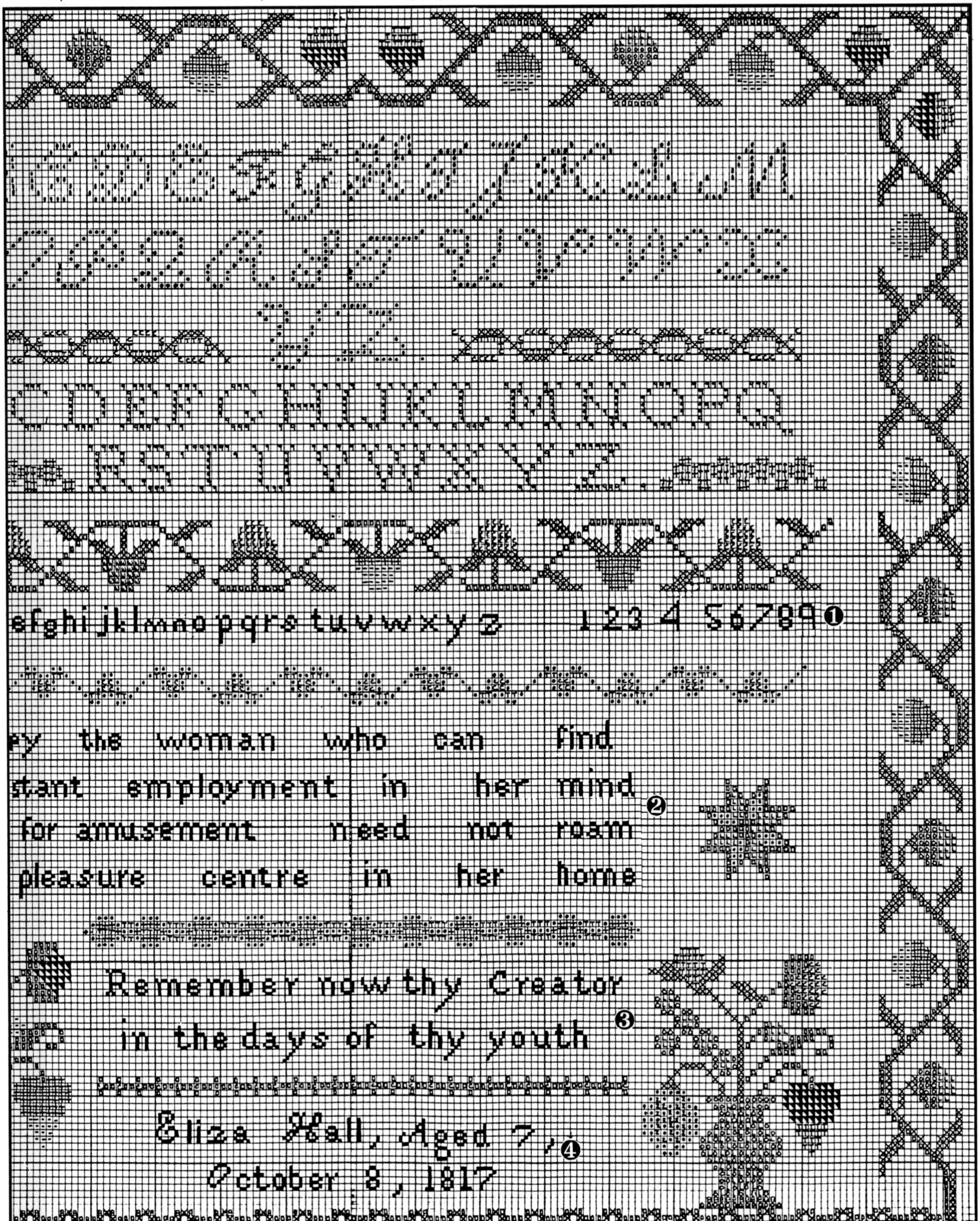

MARIA REVERE CURTIS

Paul Revere's great-granddaughter shows unusual skill at age eleven.

 Maria, born in 1808, was the second of eight children of David Curtis and Sally Revere. Her great-grandfather was Paul Revere (1743–1818), the famous silversmith, engraver, and patriot. Paul Revere and his first wife, Sarah Orne, named their second child Paul, Jr. That son was Maria's grandfather.

Maria's sampler is unusually ambitious, especially for an eleven-year-old child. Note the tree that changes from over-one to over-two threads. She chose to work on a very large piece of unevenweave linen, and she worked a great many over-one stitches—a combination that demands a patient hand and respect for fine detail—traits she might have inherited from her great-grandfather.

Collection of Paul Revere Memorial Association, Boston, Massachusetts.

ABCDEFSHIJKLMNOPQRS
TUVWXYZ · AEIOUWY · aeiouwy

abcdefghijklmnopqrstuv
wxyz

1234567891011 12

ABCDEFGHIJKLMNOPQRS
UVW

Jesus permit thy gracious name to stand
As the first effort of an infant hand
And while her fingers o'er this canvass move
Engage her tender heart to seek thy love
With thy dear children let her share a part
And write thy name thyself upon her heart

XYZ

Maria Roevere Curtis Her Work
Aged 11 years January 25 . 1819

MARIA REVERE CURTIS
(17¼ x 17¼ inches)

Maria's monumental work must have been done while she was at school because it is much too challenging for a mother to supervise at home. The alphabet that surrounds the verse is a double row of stitches done over one thread of the woven linen, not over the conventional two threads. Over-ones are difficult enough on modern, evenly woven fabric, but on uneven-weave linen like hers it is very difficult to keep the stitches even. The thread count of the original is 35- by 28-count, but beginners should work this sampler on 35-count evenweave.

The General Instructions in the Appendix show how to find the starting point and work the stitches.

Maria had to fudge her border a bit to make it come out evenly on the left side. She had to lower the left basket as well to fit its shape to the contour of the border.

It takes rare patience to do a whole alphabet in over-ones on unevenweave linen, yet this eleven-year-old's stitches are perfectly uniform.

MATERIALS
23¼ x 23¼ inches of 35-count ivory linen, dyed with the #2, 3, and 4 Coffee recipes (see Appendix); DMC embroidery floss as shown in the Chart Key (note variations in the number of strands); size 26 tapestry needle.

DIRECTIONS
After purchasing evenweave linen, pull out seven horizontal threads per inch, as evenly spaced as possible. Anchor the end of each thread in the three-inch margin. To duplicate the color of the original linen, dye it darker down the right side than on the left. Leave the upper left hand corner very light and the area around the verse almost white.

Work the sampler in cross stitch over one or two threads using two strands unless noted otherwise. Work the sawtooth border in satin stitch.

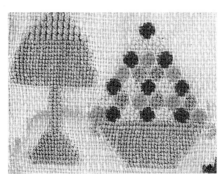

Maria Curtis and Hannah Atkins lived 90 miles apart and stitched their samplers within ten years of each other, yet both put trees in their samplers and both used the same verse.

CHART KEY		
SYMBOL	DMC #	COLOR
T	311/312	blue/dk. blue: blend 1 str. each
F	312	dk. blue, 4 str.
I +	503	lt. blue-green:,2 str., 4 str.
O ●	502	med. blue-green: 2 str., 4 str.
X	3371	darkest brown-black
U Z S	926	slate blue: 2 str., 4 str., 1 str.
K ■	435	lt. brown, 4 str.
A L	738	beige, 4 str.
C	920/435	orange/lt. brown, blend: 1 str. each
3	924	teal blue

Shaded portions of charts indicate overlap with sections on facing and following pages.

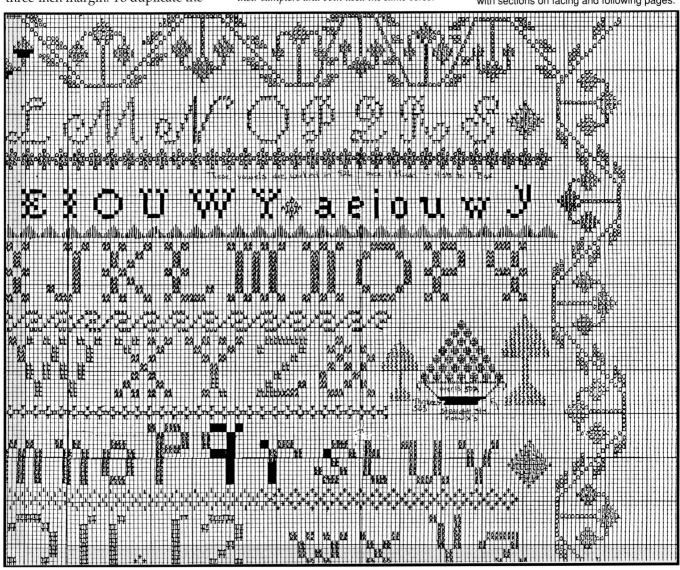

This alphabet is worked

$\mathcal{A}$ $\mathcal{B}$ $\mathcal{C}$ $\mathcal{D}$ $\mathcal{E}$ $\mathcal{F}$ $\mathcal{G}$ $\mathcal{H}$ $\mathcal{I}$ $\mathcal{K}$ $\mathcal{L}$
$\mathcal{U}$ $\mathcal{V}$ $\mathcal{W}$

Jesus permit thy gracious
As the first effort of a
And while her fingers o er
Engage her tender heart
With thy dear children le
And write thy name thyse

Maria Roevere Curti
Aged 11 years

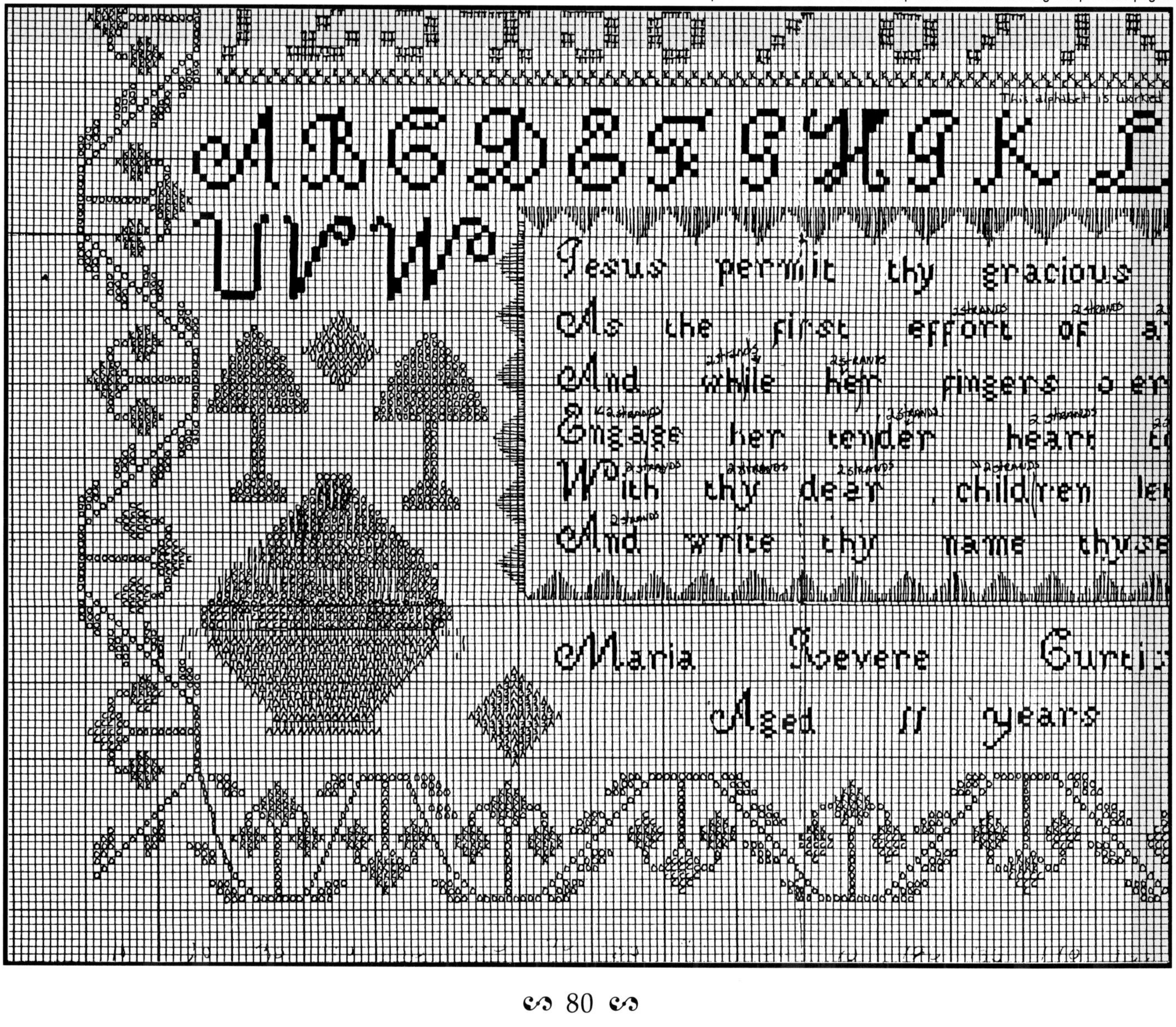

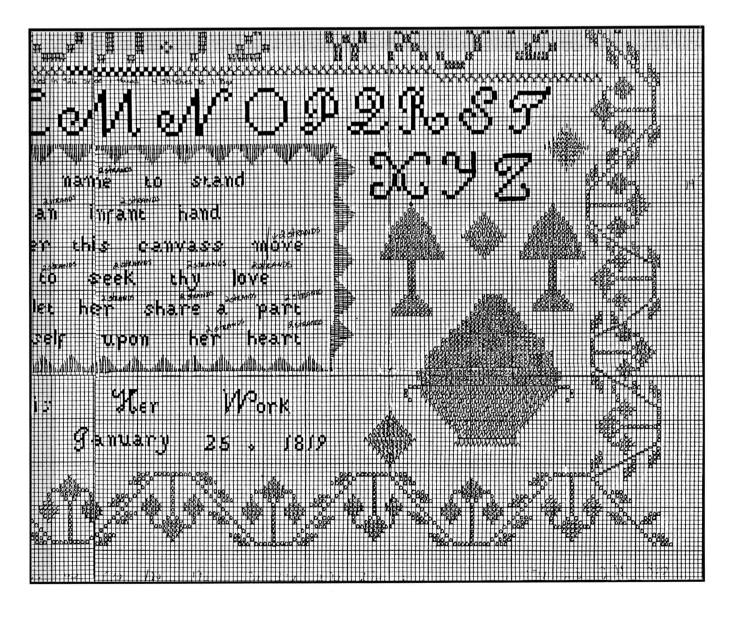

ELIZA ANN SHOWMAN

Her rococo stitch resembles the striking flame stitch in needlepoint.

 We learn from Eliza's sampler that she finished it at the age of fourteen in Sharpsburg, Maryland (the site of the famous Civil War battle of Antietam). We cannot know exactly what year that was because sometime later, when she grew old enough to be embarrassed by her age, Eliza removed the last two numbers from the date to prevent anyone who might see her sampler from calculating her present age.

By the time she was fourteen it is likely that she had already completed at least one other sampler. Her repertoire of stitches also attests to her experience. In the border she cleverly replicated a needlepoint flame stitch with rococo stitches by turning her work sideways to insert the blue center stitches between the conventional peach stitches.

ABCDEF GHIKM NNOPRS
STUVWXYZ abcdefghijk

ABCDEFGHIJKLMNOPQR
STUVWXYZ ,., abcdefghijk

ELMNOPQRSTU

Eliza Ann Showmans work done in the 14 year of her age April 22

That which fragrance is to the rose, modesty is to youth and beauty

Sharpsburg Md 18

This enlargement of the undulating border that Eliza placed across the bottom portion of the sampler uses rococo stitches only. Eliza made it look like the flame stitch was done in needlepoint by working the top and bottom rows in the usual way, then rotating her linen ninety degrees when she sandwiched the center row of blue stitches.

ELIZA ANN SHOWMAN
(17 ¼ x 16 ½ inches)

Some of Eliza's colors have faded. If you prefer to try to replicate her original palette, the floral border was carnation pink and the blue alphabet much brighter. The colors in the arresting rococo border that snakes across the lower portion of the sampler are still bright on the right end but have faded toward the left.

The General Instructions in the Appendix show how to find the starting point and work the stitches.

MATERIALS
23¼ x 22½ inches of 26-count cream linen, dyed with the #2 Coffee recipe (see Appendix); DMC embroidery floss as shown in the Chart Key (note variations in number of strands); size 24 tapestry needle.

DIRECTIONS
The original sampler is 26-count by 23-count. Work most of this sampler in cross stitch, but Eliza also uses the four-sided stitch, eyelet stitch, rice stitch and rococo stitch. To recreate the original unevenweave using 26-count evenweave, clip three vertical threads per inch across the center of the fabric, for 17¼ inches. Pull the outer end of each clipped thread until it is drawn almost free. Tack the clipped end into border of the fabric.

Refer to the footnote numbers on the chart as follows:

1: Four-sided stitch: #3064, first band; #502, second band. Alphabet #502, first row; #754 second row.

2: Eyelet stitch.

3: Rice stitch: #502 ▨; #827 ▨.

4: Rococo stitch.

CHART KEY		
SYMBOL	DMC #	COLOR
▮	3021	dk. brown: verse, name, date, 1 str.
Z	353	dk. peach
✛	754	med. pink
◪	503	lt. blue-green
X	502	med. blue-green
S	3053	moss green
◤ ●	3064	rose: 4 str., 2 str.
◀	948	flesh
E H ◼	951	med. flesh: 1 str., 2 str., 4 str.
∧	827	blue

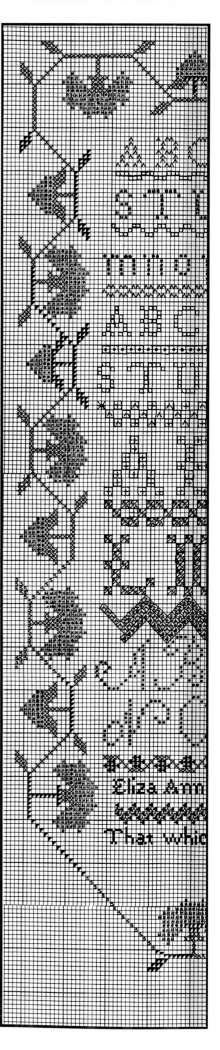

GEORGE EISENBREY

His workmanlike marking sampler was a lesson in patience for a boy.

 Rarely were boys required to stitch at all, much less make a sampler. For them, needlework was either a punishing lesson in patience, as it probably was for George, or a pastime during illness. George was about nine years old in 1826, the year our nation celebrated the fiftieth anniversary of its declaration of independence from Britain. It was also a tragic year. On that July 4th, two former presidents, Thomas Jefferson and John Adams, died within hours of each other.

George stitched his marking sampler more skillfully than did many of the girls of his time, though his borders waver slightly. His personality peeks through in small ways. Impatience may account for the four tiny mends in the linen done with rust-colored thread. Were the first two letters of his lowercase alphabet stitched so heavily because he liked the color? Or was he trying to hide a mistake? As he reached the end of his work, the last two numbers of the date—and his spirits—appear to have soared in unison.

Collection of Daughters of the American Revolution, Constitution Hall, Washington, D.C.

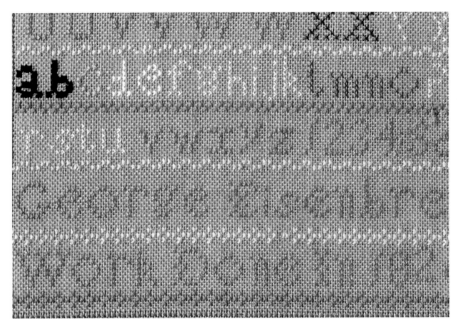

George produced a simple marking sampler without adornment. It is surprising that he was as competent a stitcher as his work demonstrates. There is little doubt that this was not only his first, but his only sampler, and that it was done as an exercise since a boy would not be expected to initial household linens later in his life. For that reason samplers done by boys are very rare indeed.

GEORGE EISENBREY

(7 ¾ x 7 ¼ inches)

Housed in the Daughters of the American Revolution Museum in Washington, D.C., George's sampler has been relatively well-preserved. It shows slight disintegration in the threads used to stitch the lowercase letters **p** and **q** in the fifth row. Since his ground was homespun his threads may have come from a local dye pot, and acid in the dye has eaten them away.

Even though this sampler is somewhat easier to replicate than the others, it is better suited for experienced stitchers because of the frequently displaced stitches.

The General Instructions in the Appendix show how to find the starting point and work the stitches.

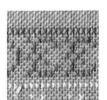

George's work is unusually well-stitched, especially for a boy, but when he had to make a few mends, he chose bright rust thread.

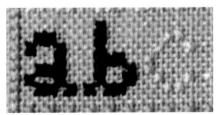

The threads George used vary in thickness and he selected a variety of colors. Very likely he had to pick through someone's mending box to find the materials to work with.

C H A R T K E Y		
SYMBOL	**DMC #**	**COLOR**
O	522	med. green, 2 str.
◖	543	beige, 1 str.
◢	612	tan, 1 str.
+	613	lt. tan, 1 str.
X	4611	Au Ver a Soie® silk, 1 str.
K	3072	lt. gray, 1 str.
−	924	teal blue, 2 str.
S	734	olive green, 2 str.
V **V**	822	off-white: 2 str., 1 str.
⌐	301	rust, 1 str.
m	367	med. green, 1 str.
v	926	slate blue, 1 str.

MATERIALS
13¾ x 13¼ inches of 25-count mocha linen, dyed with the #2 Coffee recipe (see Appendix); DMC embroidery

Shaded portions of charts indicate overlap from facing page.

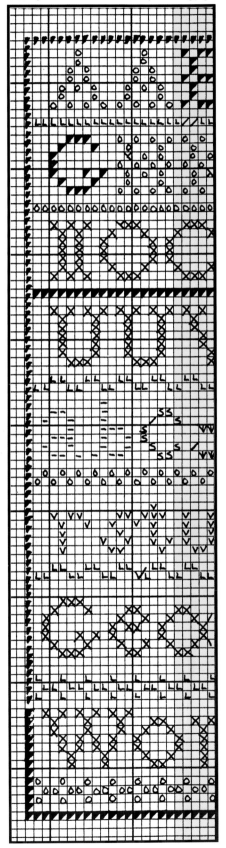

floss as shown in the Chart Key (note variations in the number of strands); size 24 tapestry needle.

DIRECTIONS

Work this entire sampler with cross stitch. Displaced stitches have made the side borders uneven. If you prefer to avoid the arduous task of repli–cating George's uneven borders as he stitched them, simply count evenly and straighten them out for him.

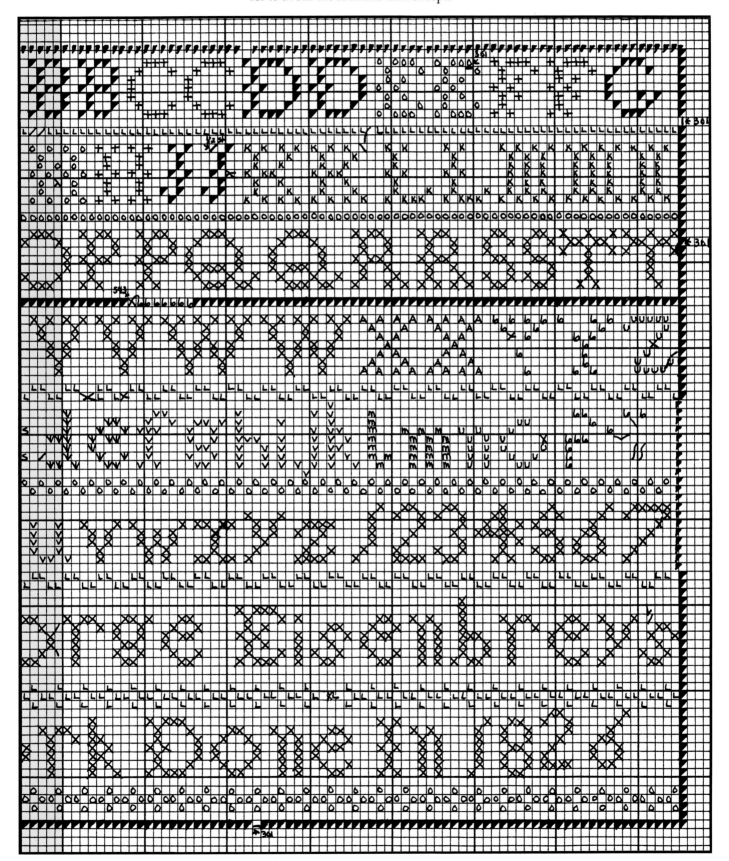

SUSANA BARTHOLOMEW

With Pennsylvania Dutch motifs, a unique "show towel" on 44-count linen.

The designs Susana worked into this item for her trousseau in 1824 are part of her Pennsylvania Dutch heritage. They decorate a large linen towel which, in the fashion of the time, was hung over common dish towels when company came. In this photograph, most of the forty inches of plain linen is folded under so that only the stitchery shows. Linen was very expensive, so the piece demonstrated not only the virtues of diligence and cleanliness, but the prosperity of her family as well.

Susana's traditional motifs are more than just ornamental. For example, the tulip represents the Trinity, the star is an ancient symbol of the deity, and the heart a symbol of love. Her sense of order apparently overshadowed her sense of self because she added an extra *W* to her name to make the line fit evenly.

Collection of Quakerstown Historical Society, Quakerstown, Pennsylvania.

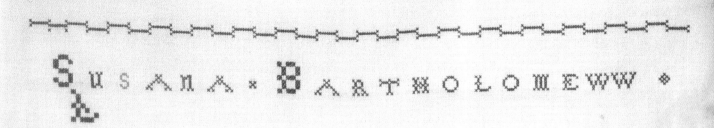

SUSANA · B ARTHOLOMEWW ·

IANUARIUS · 27 · DEN · 1824 × ⋀⋀⋀ · ◇

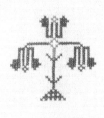  

 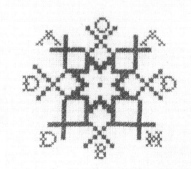 

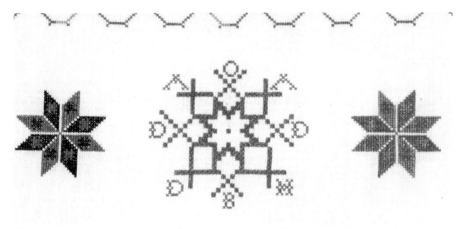

Susana used the rice stitch to work the semi-star motif in the center—a design unique to this sampler. The initials around its outer edge are likely to be those of family members.

SUSANA
BARTHOLOMEW
(15 x 40 inches)

Susana worked her show towel with meticulous care, making sure to keep her stitches within their two-thread boundaries. In what could be the first letter of a new line or a mistake, the outline of an unfinished letter remains below her name. She may not have wanted to take the time or risk clipping the threads of her linen, so she allowed the stitching to remain.

Her designs and colors are appealing. She used the rice stitch in the **B** of *Bartholomeww* and in the large motif with initials around it located in the center of the sampler.

On the previous page, the towel is shown folded so that all the decorative needlework is visible. To her original towel, Susana added approximately six inches of beautiful hand-crocheted lace at the bottom.

The General Instructions in the Appendix show how to find the starting point and work the stitches.

MATERIALS
21 x 46 inches of 44-count ivory linen; DMC embroidery floss as shown in the Chart Key; size 26 tapestry needle; hand or machine-made lace (optional).

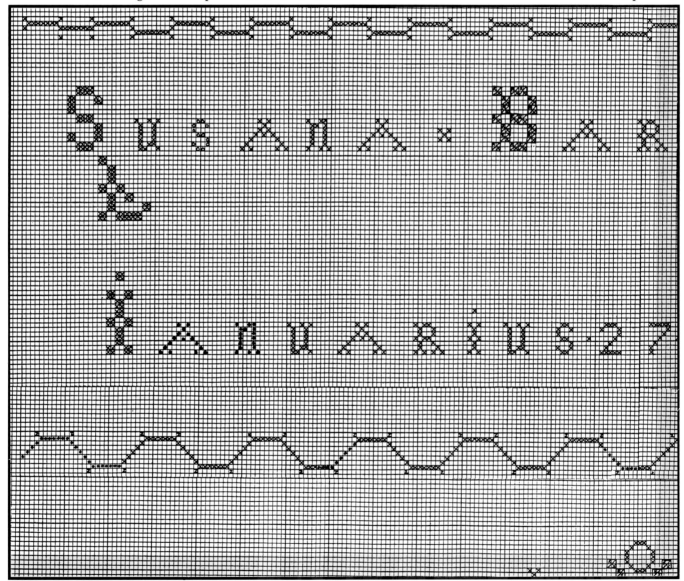

DIRECTIONS

Work all motifs in cross stitch with the exception of the large center motif and initials surrounding it, which are worked in rice stitch. Follow the arrows on the chart to locate each design. Note that Susana's dividing bands are not always straight.

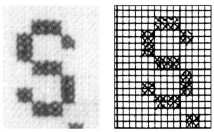

Susana did not complete the line she started under her name or, if a mistake, she chose not to snip away the threads for fear of cutting the linen or leaving telltale bits of pink thread.

*The **S** in Susana's first name is a double cross stitch to make it resemble a rice stitch, but the **B** in her surname is a real rice stitch.*

C H A R T	K E Y	
SYMBOL	**DMC #**	**COLOR**
X	3350	dk. pink
●	962	med. pink
Z	930	blue
C	931	med. blue
S	336	navy blue

Pennsylvania Dutch women used images they called "tulips" to symbolize any unknown flower encountered in the New World.

Shaded portions of chart indicate overlap with sections on facing and following pages.

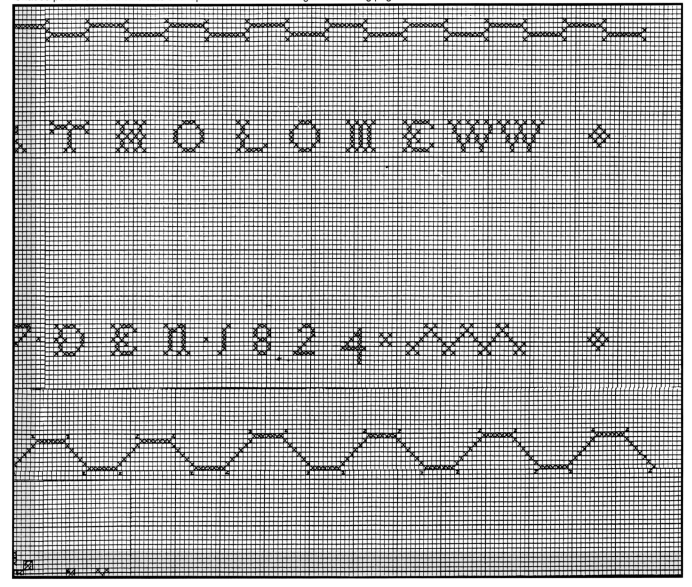

Shaded portions of chart indicate overlap with sections on facing and preceding pages.

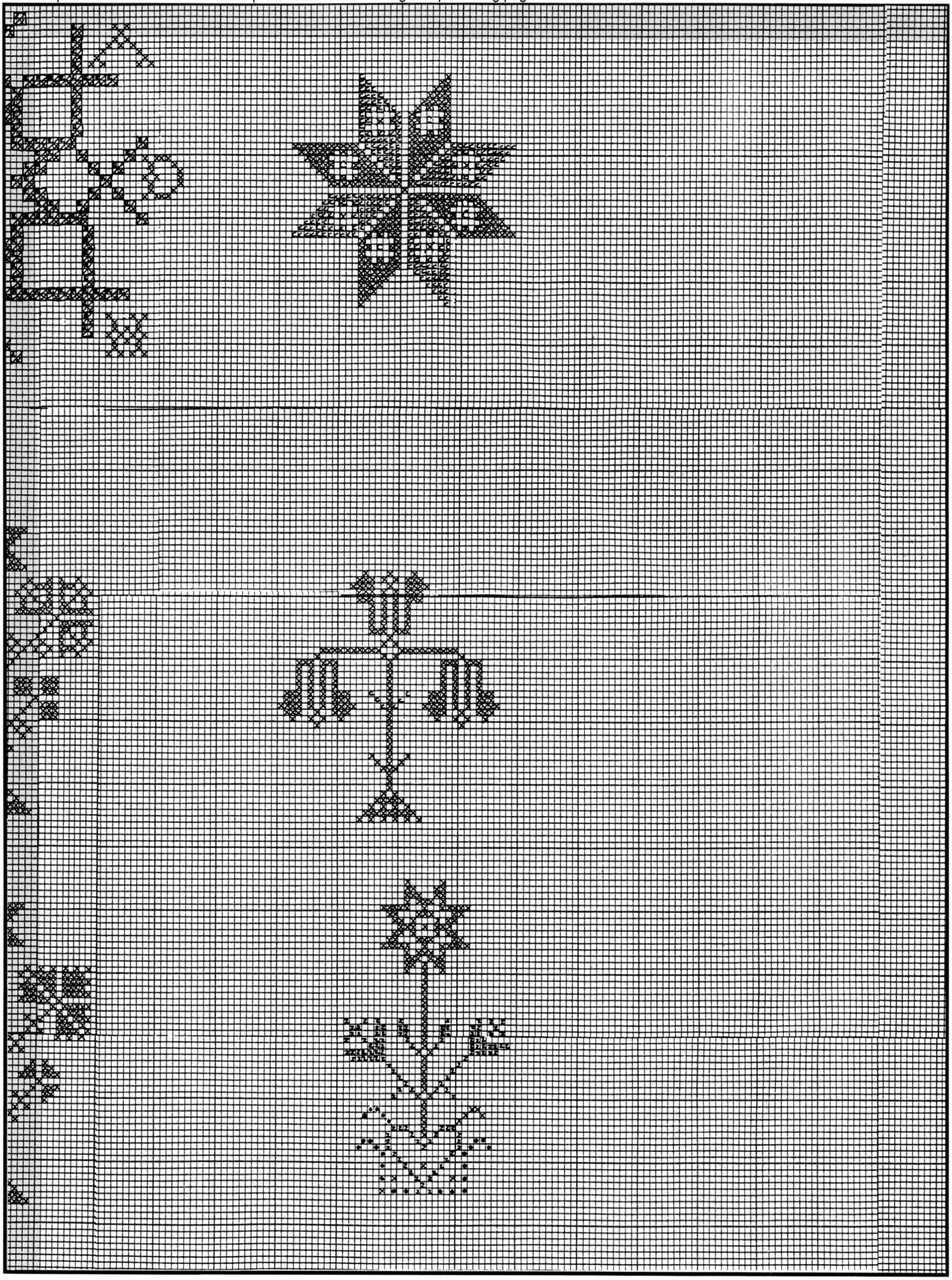

RACHEL ELLICOTT

Rosebuds, cornucopias, bluebirds, baskets, and a border of forget-me-nots.

 The Maryland town where Rachel was born was named Ellicott Mills, after her great uncle. When the mills began to close down, the town's name was changed to Ellicott City as it is known today. Rachel's mother, Mary Kirk, attended the West Town School in West Chester, Pennsylvania, a fashionable Quaker boarding school where she made two samplers.

This was Rachel's second sampler, and a considerable improvement over the first one she completed two years before, at the age of nine. The differences in the alphabets she stitched are not mistakes. Rachel copied one of them from her mother's own schoolgirl sampler stitched in 1810. Perhaps Rachel's own daughter, Mary Gilpin, in turn copied alphabets from her mother's and her grandmother's work.

Collection of Sandy Springs Museum, Olney, Maryland.

RACHEL ELLICOTT
(17 x 16¼ inches)

Rachel created an eye-catching sampler. The colors are still vibrant, as can be seen most strikingly in the cornucopia. The variety and charm of the motifs she chose make it one of the most interesting samplers of all to stitch. She offers contemporary stitchers an opportunity to learn some new stitches as well: eyelet over one thread, four-sided stitch, satin stitch, rococo stitch, and rice stitch over two threads.

The original sampler was worked on unevenweave linen that measured 18 inches (28-count) by 17 inches (30-count).

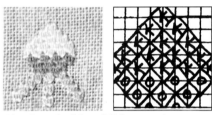

She showed off her skill by grouping rococo stitches, as shown here. It is difficult to keep them from bunching.

Rachel must have been fond of nature because she balanced formal motifs like the basket and cornucopia, which are symbols of bounty, with a gently flowing border of forget-me-nots, bluebirds, and lovely wild violets in the corners.

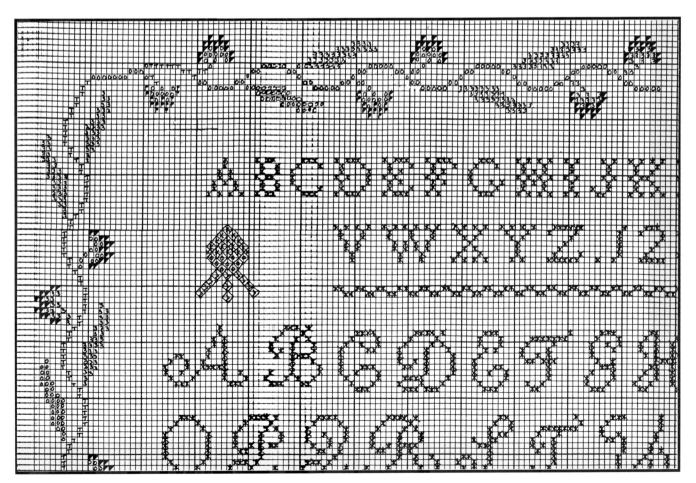

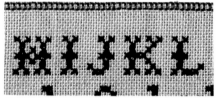

This style of alphabet was relatively modern for her time. She chose to execute it in the rice stitch over two threads instead of four.

The General Instructions in the Appendix show how to find the starting point and work the stitches.

MATERIALS

23 x 22¼ inches of 25-count cream linen, dyed with the #2 Coffee recipe (see Appendix); DMC embroidery floss as shown in the Chart Key (note variations in number of strands); size 24 tapestry needle.

This bold alphabet is a common Quaker style.

DIRECTIONS

Note that the motifs in the border do not always repeat symmetrically. Rachel also had trouble with her corners, so follow the chart carefully.

The sections of the chart on the following pages include footnote numbers. This is what those numbers mean:

1 and 2: When working the left bird with dark blue #3750, use one strand above the line and two strands below the line.

3: Work all #3750 with two strands.

4: Work the last five rococo stitches in brown thread, not black.

5: Work the darker section of the sawtooth band with two strands of brown thread.

6: Use two strands of brown thread.

7: Work the entire dividing band in a four-sided stitch.

8: Work the period in a four-sided stitch with black thread.

CHART KEY

SYMBOL	DMC #	COLOR
P	754	lt. pink
◹	758	dk. pink
K	945	lightest pink: rococo flowers
X	310	black
✳	3031	dk. brown
6	926	slate blue
◪	3750	dk. blue
•	356	rust
T	320/368	grass green/lt. green: blend 1 str. each
O	320	grass green
3	367	dk. green
▷	563/564	med. & lt. bright green: rococo flowers
E	445	yellow
▼	3045	gold
L	645	gray: periods and commas in verse
V	501	blue green

Shaded portions of charts indicate overlap from facing and following pages.

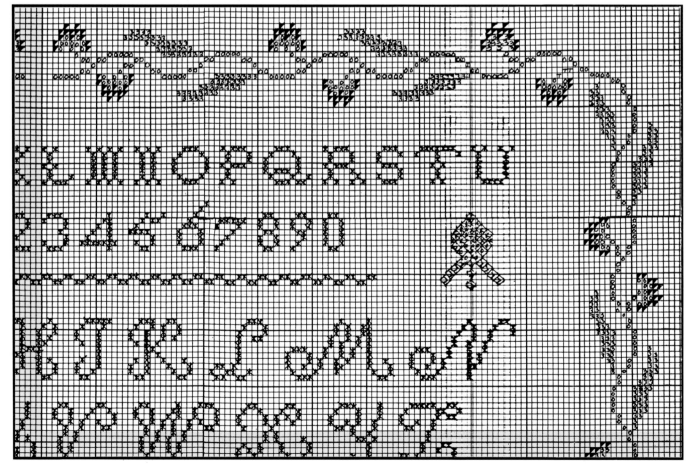

Hannah Atkins

A gentle Quaker from Cape Cod celebrates her love of nature.

Hannah Atkins was born on October 14, 1815, and was only eleven years old when she wrought her beautiful sampler. The most striking and unusual characteristic of her work is the row of trees in the center of the sampler. Her skillful stitching and choice of designs suggest that she worked under the tutelage of a teacher in Sandwich, Massachusetts, the town where she lived. The last two lines of the verse she chose can also be seen in the sampler by Maria Revere Curtis.

At the age of thirty-three, Hannah married Joseph Gregory, Jr., of Providence, Rhode Island. Their two daughters, Mary and Emma, eventually returned to Sandwich to work at the famous Sandwich Glass factory.

Collection of Sandwich Historical Society & Glass Museum, Sandwich, Massachusetts.

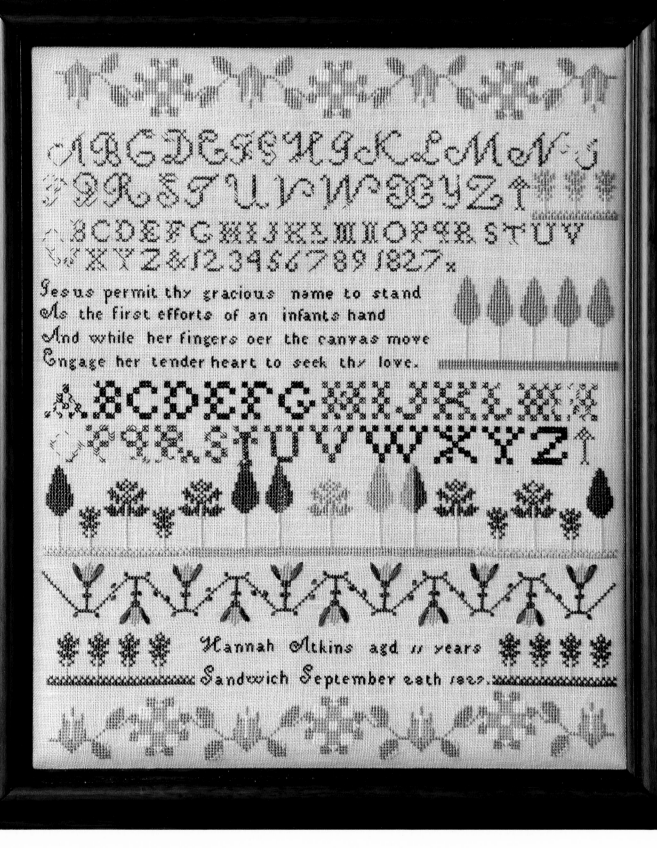

Jesus permit thy gracious name to stand
As the first efforts of an infants hand
And while her fingers oer the canvas move
Engage her tender heart to seek thy love.

Hannah Atkins agd 11 years

Sandwich September 28th 1827.

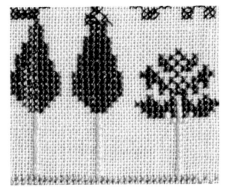

HANNAH ATKINS
(15 ¼ x 13 inches)

This Quaker child's sampler, on display in the Sandwich Glass Museum, is unusual for the sense of peacefulness it conveys. Though some stitches have begun to disappear, this is not due to any fault of Hannah's, but to the disintegration of the thread caused by acid in the dyes or exposure to light.

The General Instructions in the Appendix show how to find the starting point and work the stitches.

MATERIALS
21¼ x 19 inches of 30-count linen, dyed with the #3 Coffee recipe (see Appendix); DMC embroidery floss as shown in the Chart Key (note the number of strands shown); size 26 tapestry needle.

Hannah may have chosen both blue and green to make her tree resemble the blue spruce.

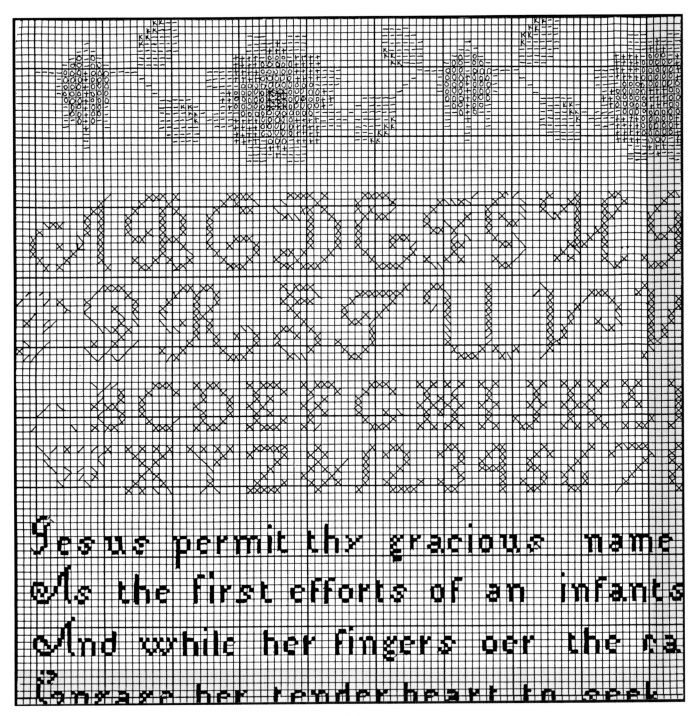

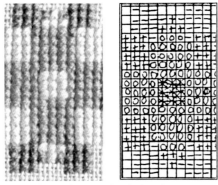

Hannah may have used a thicker thread in the center of this flower to hide a mend beneath it.

DIRECTIONS

Work the sampler in basic cross stitch except for the floral designs and leaves. Work these in a large lazy daisy stitch and fill it in with the satin stitch. This combination of stitches is a bit challenging because it must be done freehand without counting.

Work the disintegrating, partial stitches in the half-stitch, changing direction of the stitches as shown on the chart.

C H A R T K E Y		
SYMBOL	**DMC #**	**COLOR**
+ ✳	3033	beige: 2 str., 4 str.
U	524	lt. green, 2 str.
X ▮ ▮	3371	brown-black: 1 str., 2 str., 4 str.
— ✳	926	slate blue: 2 str., 1 str.
o	3045	gold, 2 str.
/	520	dark green: 2 str. plus satin stitch
↗		dk. green, 1 str.

Shaded portions of charts indicate overlap with other sections on facing and following pages.

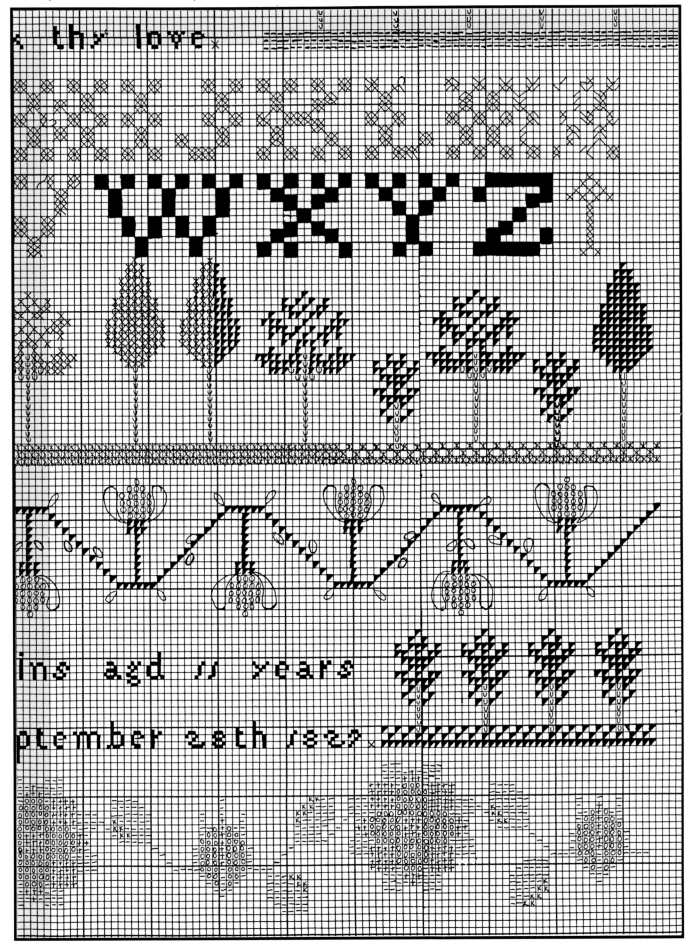

ANGELINA BROWN

A very young child executes a challenging design with a stunning border.

 Angelina was born in Richmond, Virginia, in 1821. She started this remarkably ambitious sampler when she was only seven years old, immediately after having completed at least one other equally large sampler. These two samplers are all that remain to tell us about her, since most of Richmond's genealogical records were destroyed when the city was burned by Union Soldiers in 1865.

If you look closely at the original in the Valentine Museum, you will see poignant evidence that she had so tired of the task that many times she pricked her finger and stained the linen with blood. Her impatience also shows in the rose floral border, where she stitched over two or three threads haphazardly and never crossed more than two in the same direction. The inner part of the sampler, however, is executed with great care and skill.

Collection of The Valentine Museum, Richmond, Virginia.

Although faded with time, Angelina's original colors must have been breathtaking. The beige, for example, was originally a carnation pink, and the blue would have been much brighter.

ANGELINA BROWN
(15½ x 13¼ inches)

In the framed center of this beautiful sampler, Angelina displayed unusual versatility in her use of stitches. She included feather, four-sided, satin, rice, and eyelet, which, interestingly, she worked in every hole around the frame, almost like a buttonhole.

The General Instructions in the Appendix show how to find the starting point and work the stitches.

MATERIALS
21½ x 19¼ inches of 32-count ivory linen, dyed with the #2 Coffee recipe (see Appendix); DMC embroidery floss as shown in the Chart Key; size 26 tapestry needle.

DIRECTIONS
The numbers on the chart refer to the type of stitch, whether it is worked over one or two threads, and the color to use as explained in the following footnotes:

1: Feather stitch, two strands of #739.

2: Satin stitch, two strands of #926.

3: Satin stitch, two strands of #422.

4: Work this uppercase alphabet in four-sided stitch with a single strand except for the letters **STU** which are worked with two strands of #739. Work the **ABCMNOYZ**, and heart with #524. Work the numeral **12** with #738. Work the **DEFPQR** and numerals **789** with #739. Work the **GHI** and the numeral **10** with #926. Work the **JKL** with #3045. Work the **VWX** and numeral **11** with #422.

5: Eyelet stitch with #739. The symbol "**H**" signifies that the eyelet has a visible hole. If no such symbol

is shown, do not pull the stitch tight.

6: Work this uppercase alphabet, the name, and date with one strand over one thread. Work the name, date, and uppercase **ABLMYZ** with #422. Work the **CDMO** with #524. Work the **EFUV** with #739. Work the **GHRS** with #822. Work the **JKT** with #834. Also work the lowercase alphabet with one strand over one thread. Work the **abcstu** with #822. Work the **dfpqrv** with #422. Work the **ghi** with #3768. Work the **jklw** with #738.

7: Rice stitch, two strands of #524.

8: Work this alphabet in star eyelet, except work the **Q** and **W** in regular eyelet with one strand of #336.

9: Chain stitch, one strand of #834.

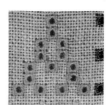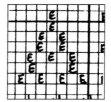

*In letters like this **A**, Angelina's stitch looks like a "button-hole" eyelet. Her stitches radiate from the center hole over every thread instead of to the four corners only.*

CHART KEY		
SYMBOL	**DMC #**	**COLOR**
X	934	dk. green
З	3768	blue
O	422	sand
C	739	lt. beige
Z	522	med. green
■	926	slate blue
K	336	navy
T	822	off-white
●	738	beige
E	3046	pale yellow
S	3045	gold

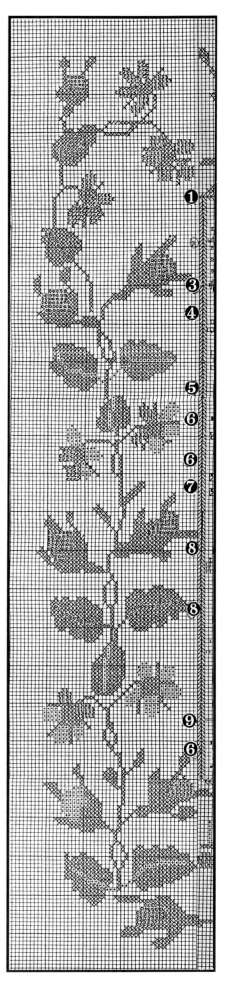

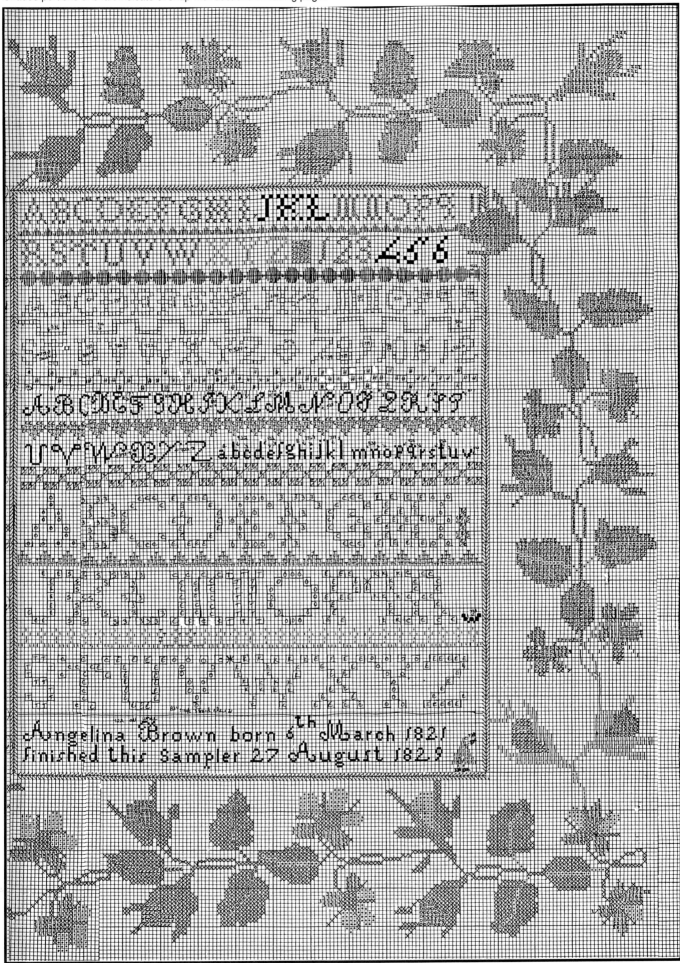

MARY E. CARPENTER

A green border, blue leaves, and roses are the signature of her schooling.

The schools that taught young girls their domestic arts and letters often tried to distinguish themselves by imposing a uniform style on the stitchery they taught. It was not Mary, therefore, who chose blue for her leaves and green for her border, or conceived the motto, "Seek Heaven." It was her school. Another sampler in the Strong Museum done by a child that same year follows the same conventions, including the wreath around the motto.

It appears that this school paid more attention to decorative motifs than the proper formation of the letters. In her first uppercase alphabet, the letters *I* and *J* are nearly the same. They are also similar in the lowercase alphabet, except for the length of their descenders. By the time she reached ten years, a girl at that time normally had completed at least two samplers. This one would have been a showpiece attesting to Mary's proper schooling.

Other samplers made at the school Mary attended in Rochester, New York, also had the same motto and blue leaves.

MARY E. CARPENTER
(16 x 14¾ inches)

Mary may have been displaying a bit of home-town pride by stitching "Rochester" into her piece. The bold green in the border seems not to have been dulled by time. It is easy to imagine how striking the effect must have been when the off-whites in the border and flowers were the same bright pink as those same threads on the back of the sampler still are where the light has not faded them.

The General Instructions in the Appendix show how to find the starting point and work the stitches.

*The number **4** is probably the best visible indicator of how bright all the colors once were.*

MATERIALS
22 x 20¾ inches of 25-count cream linen, dyed with the #2 Coffee recipe (see Appendix); DMC embroidery floss as shown in the Chart Key (note that the number of strands vary from two to four); size 24 tapestry needle.

DIRECTIONS
Except for the sawtooth border, which is worked in satin stitch, work entirely in cross stitch. Some stitches are crossed over only one thread rather than the usual two threads.

CHART KEY		
SYMBOL	**DMC #**	**COLOR**
U I	927	lt. slate blue: 2 str., 4 str.
K	3064	rose
L X V	310	black: 1 str., 2 str., 4 str.
S ■	712	off-white 4 str.
●	930	blue
◤	561	bright green
◖	613	lt. beige

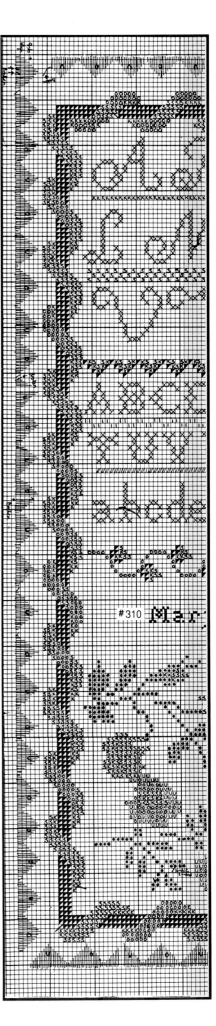

#310 Mar

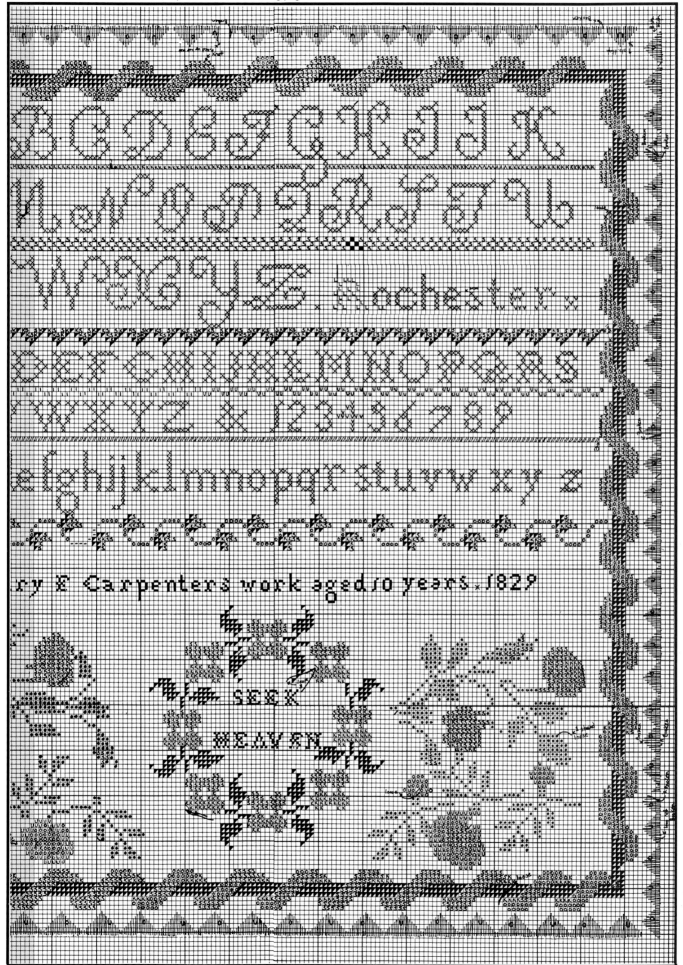

JOANN ISABELLA GIBBS

It took unusual patience for an eight-year-old to hook tambour-work florals.

Joann was born on October 18, 1820, in Sandwich, Massachusetts, the daughter of Thomas F. and Patience Gibbs. This was her second sampler, and it is a masterpiece of stitchery, especially for a child so young.

She worked the row of pale blue-green flowers in silk, crossing her threads differently here than in the rest of her piece by turning the work sideways, thus giving the flowers a different sheen. Perhaps she found it easier to stitch this way, or wanted them to attract the eye, or perhaps she did it just for fun.

The tambour floral designs are chain-stitched with one strand of silk, using a special hook and a hoop. Joann counted her threads so accurately that the stitches look machine-made.

These flowers were worked in tambour stitch and satin stitch, a combination rarely found in New England samplers. The stitching is so fine it looks as if it were done by machine.

JOANN ISABELLA GIBBS

(14⅛ x 17¼ inches)

The challenge in reproducing this unusually decorative piece is the tambour work. Tambour work is done using a tambour hook—an implement similar to a #000 crochet hook. With the fabric secured in a hoop, you can become proficient with a tambour hook after a bit of practice on scrap. However, if you prefer to omit the tambour work, the chart allows you to substitute smaller flowers done in cross stitch instead.

Joann counted one hole between each stitch, rather than each thread. You will find, as you stitch your sampler, that this method gives you better control over the constant circular direction of your stitching. If you count uniformly, your piece will have the same look as Joann's, even if the stitches are not all the same size.

The pairs of letters following the lowercase alphabet are called *ligatures*—characters consisting of two or more letters united, such as æ or fl.

The printer's *s*, which resembles ∫, was used to save space and is often found in samplers of the 1700s. The second *s* was often set in modern style.

The General Instructions in the Appendix show how to find the starting point and work the stitches.

MATERIALS

20⅛ x 23¼ inches of 32-count linen, dyed with the #1 Coffee recipe (see Appendix); DMC embroidery floss and Au Ver a Soie® silk as shown in the Chart Key (note that the pale, blue-green flowers and tambour are both worked in silk); size 26 tapestry needle; tambour hook; embroidery hoop.

DIRECTIONS

Work this sampler with two strands in cross stitch, eyelet stitch, and four-sided stitch. Work the row of pale blue-green flowers in silk. Note that they are crossed differently from the rest of the piece. To give those flowers their special sheen, rotate your work 90 degrees as you stitch.

Work the flowers in the top two corners using the eyelet stitch in the centers of the flowers and the four-sided stitch for the stems. Use the eyelet to form periods after the top two alphabets and numbers.

Work the large flower-and-basket motifs with one strand of silk in tambour and satin stitch. (If you decide to omit the tambour, work the two floral motifs in the lower corners of the chart in cross stitch instead.) To work the large flowers and basket in Sections 5 and 6, enlarge the patterns for those insets on a photocopy machine

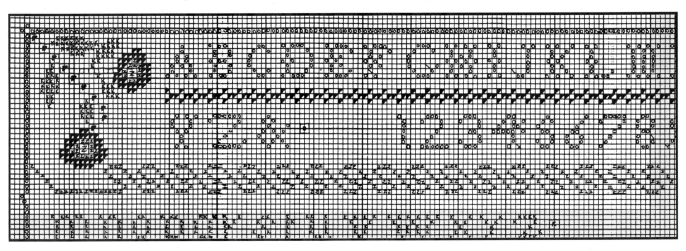

to twice the size shown. Transfer the enlarged designs onto your fabric with a transfer pen or pencil, positioning the designs as shown on the preceding page.

CHART KEY		
SYMBOL	DMC #	COLOR
K N	1814	blue: Au Ver a Soie®
O	3371	darkest brown
X	927	lt. slate blue
◣	407	pale rose
Z	822	off-white
V	928	palest slate blue

Work the light aqua-blue flowers in the border across the top section with one strand of silk, Au Ver a Soie® #1814. Turn the piece sideways while working on it to reproduce the special sheen found in the original.

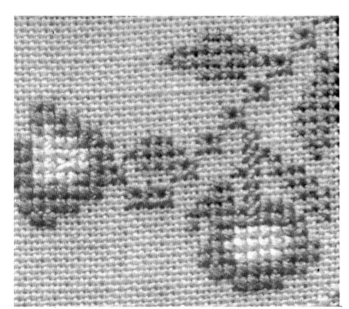

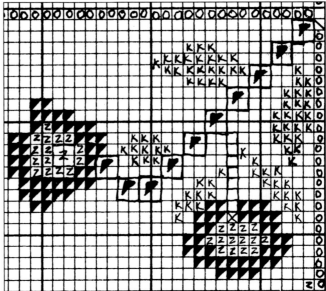

Combining different stitches within a single design motif, as Joann did so beautifully in the Cape roses at the top of her sampler, produces an appealing effect. She worked the stems with the eyelet stitch and bordered them with the four-sided stitch. Then she placed one or more eyelet stitches in the center of each rose. The end result is charming.

Shaded portion of charts indicates overlap with other sections on facing and following pages.

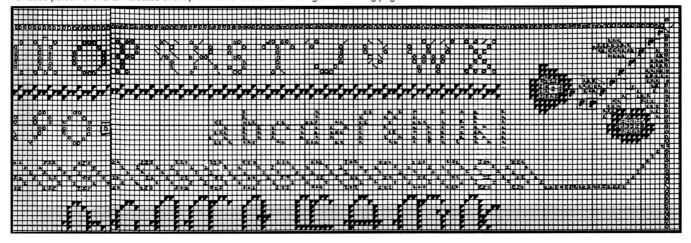

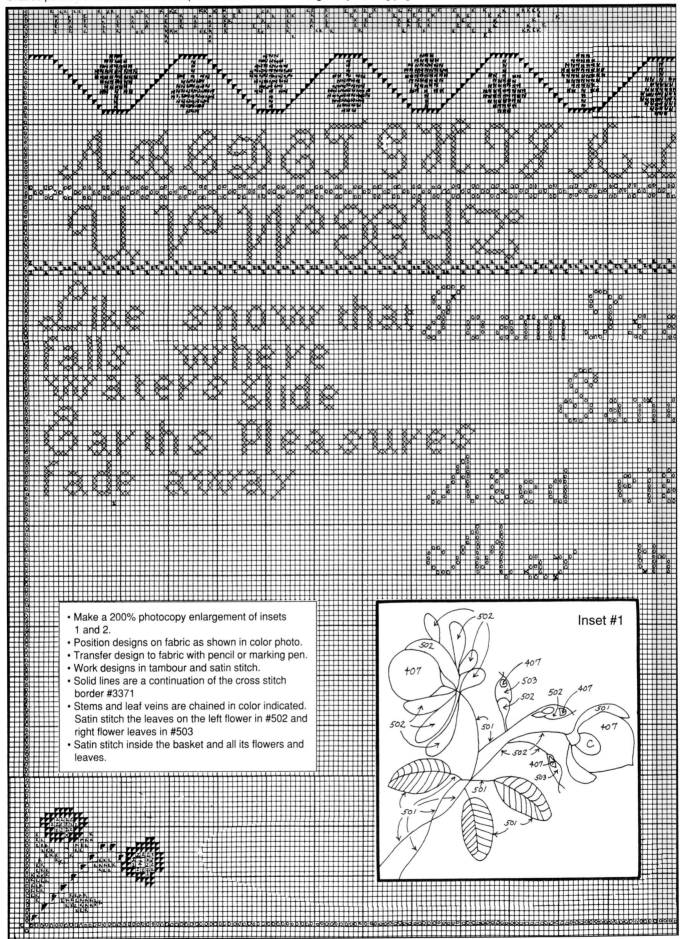

- Make a 200% photocopy enlargement of insets 1 and 2.
- Position designs on fabric as shown in color photo.
- Transfer design to fabric with pencil or marking pen.
- Work designs in tambour and satin stitch.
- Solid lines are a continuation of the cross stitch border #3371
- Stems and leaf veins are chained in color indicated. Satin stitch the leaves on the left flower in #502 and right flower leaves in #503
- Satin stitch inside the basket and all its flowers and leaves.

Inset #1

Sophia Elizabeth Kummer

A simple prayer in her seventh year, stitched at a Moravian school.

 Sophia was born on October 16, 1824, the second of five children. She was supposed to have been the "delicate" child in the family, but she lived to be 104 years old.

She and her sister Caroline were educated at the Bethlehem Female Seminary in Pennsylvania, where "Aunty Kummer" taught needlework. Letters from the girls' parents in Nazareth arrived by the mail coach once a week. In one dated 1835, their mother, Sarah, advised the girls on their choice of needlework. "Selection and arrangement," she wrote, "can be made so as to give a sufficient knowledge of the work, without being so large as to become tedious, and unnecessarily expensive."

After graduating, the two sisters opened a girls' school, which eventually failed due to their youth and inexperience. They both became governesses for private families where, presumably, they taught fine needlework to the children under their care.

Collection of Moravian Museum, Bethlehem, Pennsylvania.

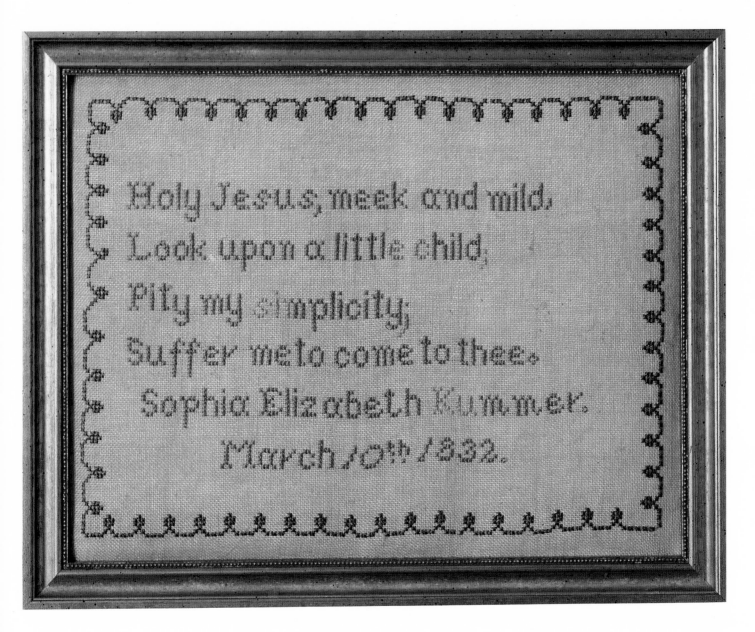

Holy Jesus, meek and mild,
Look upon a little child,
Pity my simplicity;
Suffer me to come to thee.
Sophia Elizabeth Kummer.

March 10th 1832.

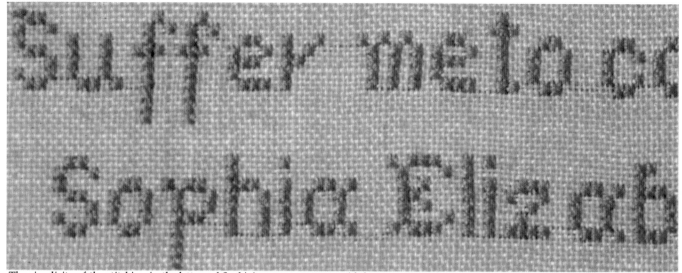

*The simplicity of the stitching in the letters of Sophia's prayer contrasts with her more ornately stitched name, as in the letters **mm** in **Kummer** and the **th** in **Elizabeth** seen on the facing page.*

SOPHIA ELIZABETH KUMMER
(10¼ x 7½ inches)

Sophia was born on October 16, 1824, in Bethlehem, Pennsylvania. She was the second of five children of the Reverend John Gottlob Kummer and Sarah Hinchcliffe Kummer. After graduating from a Moravian school for girls, she and her sister opened a school of their own. When it failed, both girls found work as governesses to private families. An old school friend introduced Sophia to the Peirce family. On her thirty-second birthday, October 16, 1856, she and Edward Peirce were married in Baltimore, Maryland.

The General Instructions in the Appendix show how to find the starting point and work the stitches.

MATERIALS
16¼ x 13½ inches of 30-count linen, dyed with the #3 Coffee recipe; DMC embroidery floss as shown in the Chart Key; size 24 tapestry needle.

DIRECTIONS
Work all the letters in cross stitch over two threads using two strands of floss. Work the periods placed at the ends of lines and under the **th** in **10th** with four-sided stitches.

Shaded portion of chart indicates overlap with facing page.

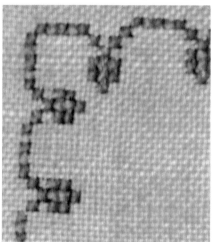

Sophia's borders seem to have had minds of their own as shown in this photo-enlargement of the top left corner.

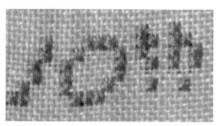

*By placing periods under the **th** with two four-sided stitches, she has drawn attention to the date she completed her labors.*

CHART KEY		
SYMBOL	DMC #	COLOR
O	3750	dk. blue
✳	613	lt. beige
✕	612	beige

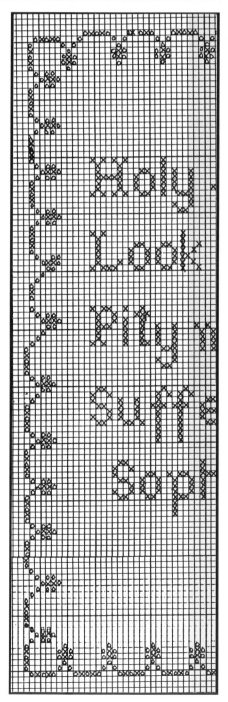

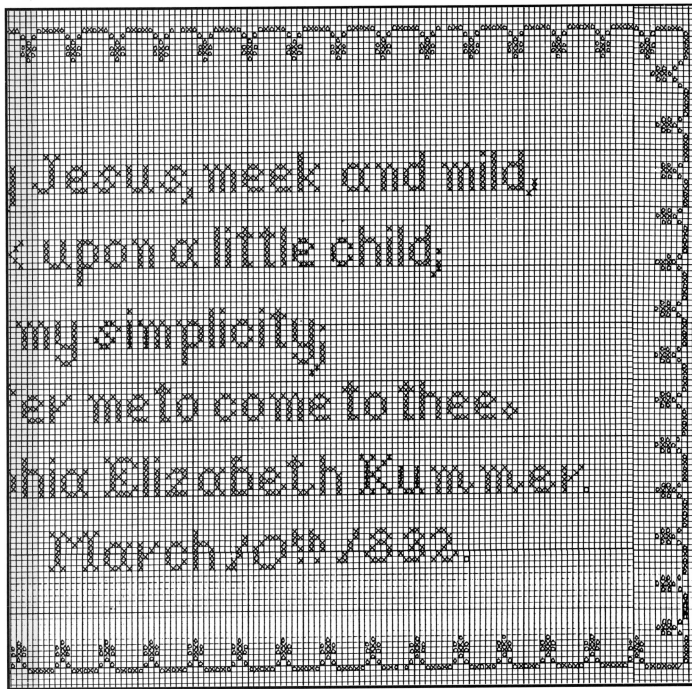

Jesus meek and mild,
upon a little child,
my simplicity
er me to come to thee.
hia Elizabeth Kummer.
March 10th 1832.

RUTH & RUBY STRATTON

Ruby had to finish the work, so she added two motifs to outshine her twin.

 This brightly colored sampler was created jointly by ten-year-old twins, each embroidering one half. Differences in their skill (and enthusiasm) can be seen when examining the sampler closely. Ruby, the younger twin and the better stitcher, had to wait until her sister finished her part, but then added the two flowers in over-ones at the end of the alphabet as an extra flourish.

Ruth and Ruby were born in Bennington, Vermont, on December 9, 1833, to Freeman Stratton and Thankful Harringon Stratton. Their father was a well-respected farmer and a lifelong resident of Bennington. Their mother was related to the Galusha family that settled in Shaftsbury, Vermont.

There were several Bennington-area educational institutions that Ruth and Ruby could have attended, including Reverend Preston's Boarding and Day School for Young Ladies, which offered instruction in English, French, drawing, painting, and ornamental needlework.

Collection of Bennington Museum, Bennington, Vermont.

ABCDEFGHIJKLM
NOPQRSTUVWXYZ
abcdefghijklmn
opprstuvwxyz

The · kind thing · is
the · right thing

1234567890

Ruth
Stratton
December
Ninth
1833

Ruby
Stratton
December
Ninth
1833

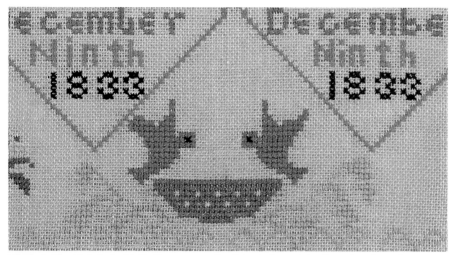

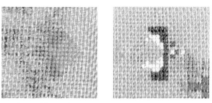

The twin bluebirds in the birdbath appear to echo the twin hearts joined together above them.

RUTH AND RUBY STRATTON
(15¼ x 11 inches)

Ruth was a school teacher before her marriage in 1858 to Heman Rockwood. They had four children: Sheldon, Elmer, Walter, and Alice. Ruth also taught Sunday school for twenty years at the Methodist Church in Bennington, Vermont. She died in Bennington in 1910, at the age of 77.

Ruby, Ruth's twin, lived with her parents until her marriage in 1855 to Solomon Howard. She then moved to his farm in South Shaftsbury. They also had four children: Ruth, Freeman, Murilla, and Rollin. Ruby died in 1924 at the age of 91.

It is puzzling why the twins' mother or teacher cut the linen horizontally and gave each child half, since each piece is certainly large enough to make two respectable samplers. As the older twin, Ruth started the stitching, working from the top left corner to the center of the

Ruth worked this quarter first.	Ruby worked this quarter second.
Ruth worked this quarter second.	Ruby worked this quarter first.

The twins stitched different portions of the sampler at different times, as shown above.

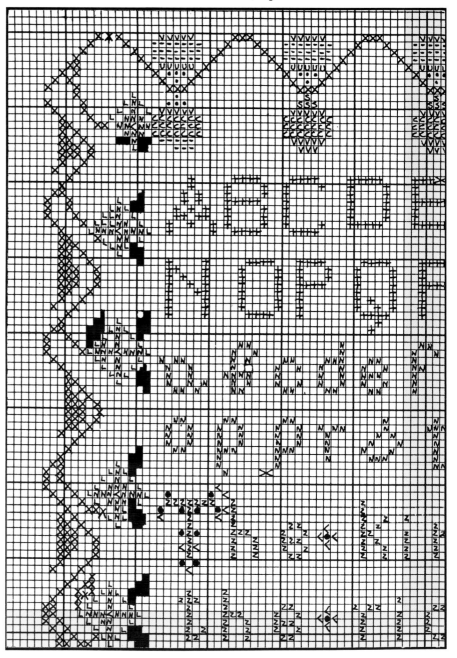

linen. Ruby took over and had to finish the alphabets, perhaps against her will. That may explain why she inserted two little flowers in over-one stitches. She may have been trying to assert the value of her contribution.

As you work on this sampler

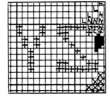

Ruby got her letter Z backwards, as many schoolchildren still do.

you will see many other instances where the sisters expressed their individuality. Look for two different interpretations of the same motifs.

The General Instructions in the Appendix show how to find the starting point and work the stitches.

MATERIALS
21¼ x 17 inches of 25-count mocha linen, dyed with the #2 Coffee recipe (see Appendix); DMC embroidery floss as shown in the Chart Key (note different symbols for any variations in number of strands); size 24 tapestry needle.

Ruby worked the bottom half of the linen first and stitched the flower on the right. Later, Ruth took over and did the flower on the left.

DIRECTIONS
Although you work this sampler entirely in cross stitch, work some stitches over only one thread instead of the usual two threads.

Shaded portions of charts indicate overlap with sections on facing and following pages.

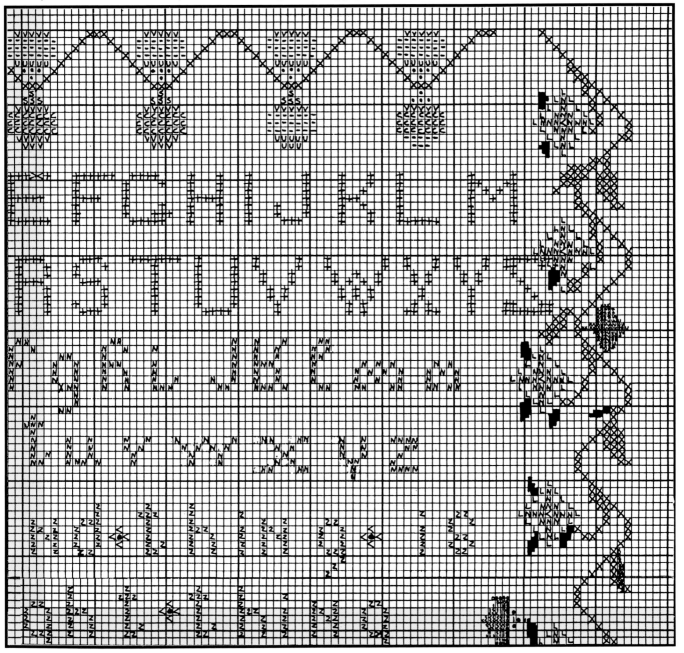

CHART KEY

SYMBOL	DMC #	COLOR
Z	310	black
+	517	bright blue
X	320	grass green
N	920	orange
II	904	dk. bright-green
●	989	lt. green
U	776	pink
<	783	gold
L	209	purple
I	610	drab brown
K	939	dk. navy
S	924	teal blue
•	775	baby blue
▲	761	salmon pink
c	822	off-white
V	738	beige
−	420	sand
Δ	370	olive green
3	936	dk. forest green
c	822	mend, off-white

ESTHER ELIZABETH HISTED

Soft colors, flowing letters, and three baskets—but, sadly, left unfinished.

Esther was born in northern Erie County, Pennsylvania, in about 1822 and died at the age of sixteen before completing this sampler. One can see that the last stitches in the bottom border were beginning to wander. Fortunately, she put her initials in the fourth row so that she may be properly credited for her skill, which she demonstrated especially in the three floral baskets. She had a delicate sense of color which can be appreciated today. After her death, her sampler must have been rolled up and put away untouched by light for 150 years. As a result, the colors live on. Her family must have been relatively prosperous to provide her with a large piece of 44-count linen and such a varied palette of colors—pale slate blue, gold, blue-greens, rich brown, warm rose, and a touch of bright red. Had she lived she could have studied art at Oberlin which, in the year she died, was the first college to open its doors to women.

Collection of Museum of Fine Arts, Boston, Massachusetts.

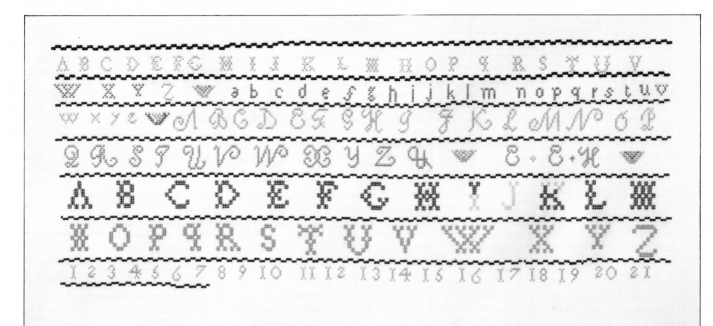

The three baskets located approximately 3¾ inches below the last border seem to be floating in space. It was not unusual to stitch the decorative motifs before filling in the verse or other stitching. Whimsically, Esther made the two side baskets different by changing the color of a bird.

ESTHER ELIZABETH HISTED
(18 x 19 inches)

Esther died before she was able to complete her work. She stitched her initials in cursive capitals at the end of the fourth row, but she probably planned to add her full name, age, and the date at the bottom of the piece as was the tradition. It would, however, be unusual to see both initials and a full name. The original, still unframed, was worked on very light linen that has not darkened appreciably with age; however, there is a large stain at the bottom.

The General Instructions in the Appendix show how to find the starting point and how to work the stitches.

MATERIALS
24 x 25 inches of 44-count ivory linen; DMC embroidery floss as shown in the Chart Key (note variation in number of strands in #502, #3371, and #407); size 26 tapestry needle.

DIRECTIONS
Stitch the entire piece in cross stitch over two threads. To place baskets, refer to the asterisks in the charts located near the numerals **1**, **2**, and **3** and the letters **a**, **b**, and **c**.

From ***1**, found near the end of the bottom unfinished band, measure 3½ inches down to locate ***a** at the top of the left basket. After working that

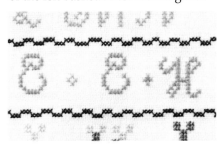

E E H, Esther Elizabeth Histed, did not want for resources. She was given an unusually large piece of linen and apparently had access to as much of any color as she needed.

basket, measure 3¼ inches from ***2** to the right to locate ***b**. After working the center basket, measure 3½ inches from ***3** to the right to locate ***c**, where the right-hand basket starts. In the original the bottom is hemmed. Measure down from the bottom of the baskets 6¼ inches of plain linen, including a ¼-inch hem.

CHART KEY		
SYMBOL	**DMC #**	**COLOR**
+	927	lt. slate blue, 1 str.
X ◪	502	blue-green: 1 str., 2 str.
L	504	light blue-green
= ■	3371	darkest brown: 1 str., 2 str.
•	347	red
◢	833	gold
O •	407	lt. rose: 1 str., 2 str.
✳	992	bright green

Shaded portions of chart indicate overlap with sections on facing and following pages.

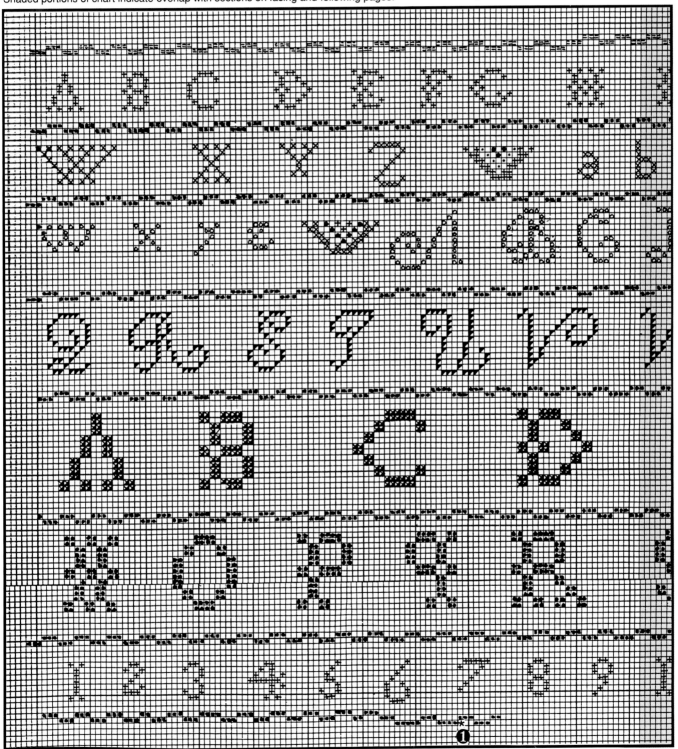

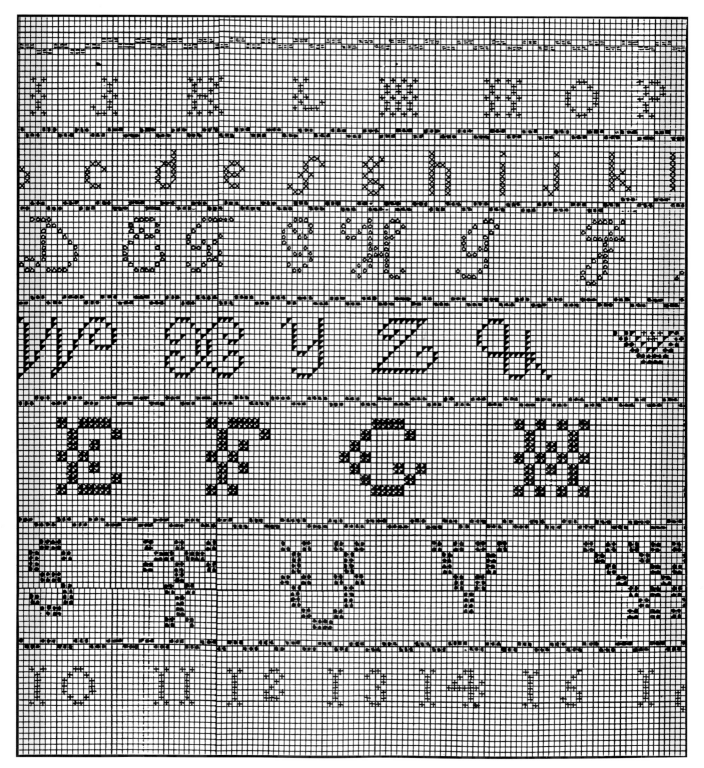

Shaded portions of chart indicate overlap with sections on facing and preceding pages.

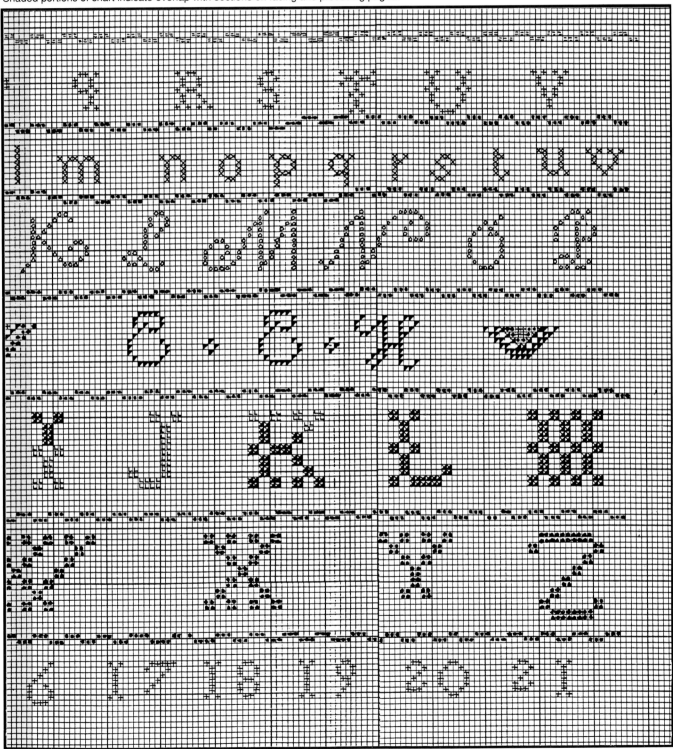

ELIZABETH GIBSON

Southern girls worked a variety of stitches. She even invented one.

 Although Elizabeth did not date her work, it can be dated about 1850, the year Senator Henry Clay of Kentucky negotiated the famous Missouri Compromise. Elizabeth did not compromise; she planned carefully and executed a classic marking sampler, demonstrating with a practiced hand a wide variety of stitches. The one she invented, perhaps unwittingly, is the pink "filling" stitch in the second border from the bottom.

Among the points of interest in this work are the backwards *J*s in the top two alphabets. The *J* was done correctly in the bottom alphabet, which is composed of demanding eyelet stitches over only one thread. In the lowercase version, her *J* sits on the line rather than descending as it should. She wisely deployed her numbers to fill out lines, but carelessly tied off threads and left them hanging. The color in her name has faded almost to white but was probably bright pink originally.

Collection of The Valentine Museum, Richmond, Virginia.

L
MNOPQRSTUV
WXYZ&1234567
abcdefghiklmnop
qrstuvwxyz8910
ABCDEFGHIJKL
MNOPQRSTUV
WXYZ12345678

ELIZABETH GIBSON

(9½ x 6¾ inches)

The variety of stitches Elizabeth used suggests that she had considerable experience, so this is not likely to have been her first sampler. In general, girls who lived in the Southern states during this period were taught to use a wider variety of stitches in their samplers than girls from the Northern states were. They were also taught to be more meticulous. The backs of needlework executed in the Southern states tend to be neater. By replicating this sampler an intermediate stitcher may add a variety of new stitches to her repertoire.

The General Instructions in the Appendix show how to find the starting point and work the stitches.

MATERIALS

15½ x 12¾ inches of 25-count mocha linen, dyed with the #2 Coffee recipe (see Appendix); DMC embroidery floss as shown in the Chart Key (note any variations in number of strands); size 24 tapestry needle.

DIRECTIONS

Work this sampler with two strands of floss except where the Chart Key or a footnote indicates a different number of strands.

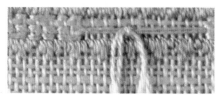

It is difficult to tell whether Elizabeth created this stitch, or was simply tying up loose ends.

CHART KEY		
SYMBOL	DMC #	COLOR
X ✖	310	black: 2 str., single thread
● O	407	pale rose: 2 str., single thread
H	320	grass green, 2 str.
◼ V	612	beige: 1 str., single thread

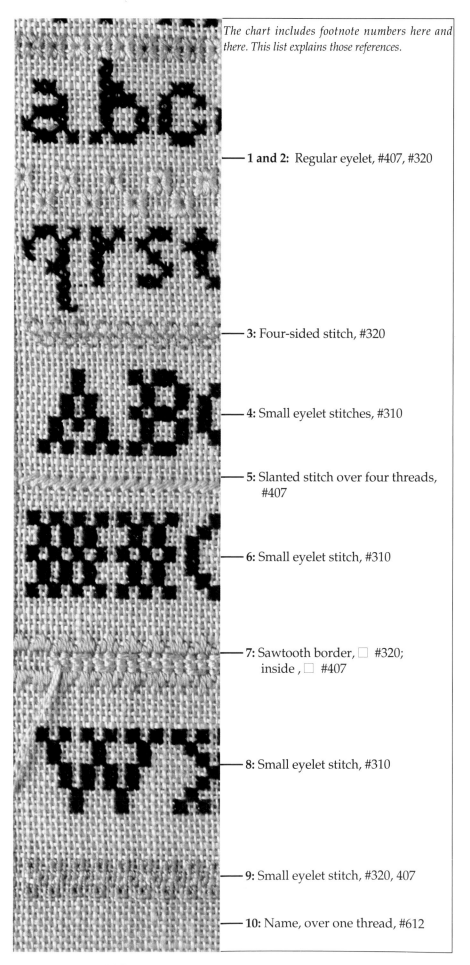

The chart includes footnote numbers here and there. This list explains those references.

1 and 2: Regular eyelet, #407, #320

3: Four-sided stitch, #320

4: Small eyelet stitches, #310

5: Slanted stitch over four threads, #407

6: Small eyelet stitch, #310

7: Sawtooth border, ☐ #320; inside, ☐ #407

8: Small eyelet stitch, #310

9: Small eyelet stitch, #320, 407

10: Name, over one thread, #612

MARY JANE HILLS

She completed her Victorian marking sampler as the Civil War began.

 No records remain to tell us how old Mary Jane was when she completed her work. Judging by the quality of her stitching, and by the fact that it is a marking sampler, this was probably her first. Most girls in the mid-19th century completed their first sampler by the time they were ten years old.

Marking samplers are seldom decorative, although Mary Jane bound hers with a pretty blue ribbon to keep its edges from fraying. They stick to their alphabets because they are utilitarian works that will be referred to later in life to copy letters from when marking household linens. It is unlikely that Mary Jane came from a poor family because the 35-count linen she used almost certainly had to be imported. Time has turned it the rich color of parchment, and the originally bright hues of her threads have mellowed with age.

Collection of Old York Historical Society, York, Maine.

A B C D E F G H I J K L M N O P Q R S T U V W X Y Z 1 2 3 4 5 6 7 8 9 10 a b c d e f g h i j k l m n o p q r s t u v w x y z . 1 2 3 4 5 6 7 8 9 10 11 12 13 14 15

Mary Jane Mills June 1861.

*The stitching in Mary Jane's capital letters had to be perfect because she did two of each and mistakes would show. The letter **J** was frequently omitted from uppercase alphabets even as late as 1861. Her ribbon border prevents the edges from fraying and allows the sampler to be rolled up and stored. Rolling was not only economical (frames were very expensive), it also prevented sunlight from fading the colors.*

MARY JANE HILLS
(6½ x 6½ inches)

The most striking part of Mary Jane's marking sampler is the blue ribbon border. On the original it appears that she had hurriedly stitched it in place. Other than that, her work is neat and disciplined. The only disintegration of the original is in the #3371 border.

Mary Jane worked her marking sampler entirely in cross stitch except for a running stitch holding down the blue border. Hers is not a difficult piece to reproduce, and the ribbon border makes it almost irresistible.

The General Instructions in the Appendix show to find the starting point and work the stitches.

MATERIALS

12½ x 12½ inches of 35-count ivory linen, dyed with Perfection Dye® Old Ivory (see Appendix); DMC embroidery floss and Au Ver a Soie® silk as shown in the Chart Key (note variations in number of strands); size 26 tapestry needle; 1 yard of ½-inch ribbon to match #336 floss for border; ¼ yard of ¼-inch ribbon of the same color for the bow.

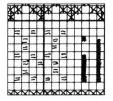

In an effort to make her somewhat plain marking sampler a little fancier, Mary Jane used a dressy, over-one alphabet in lowercase letters.

DIRECTIONS

Work the entire sampler with one strand of thread, except for #336.

To form the border and bow, fold the ½-inch ribbon over the edge of the fabric so that ¼ inch of the ribbon shows on the front and ¼ inch on the back. Position the ribbon so that the two ends meet in the middle at the top. Pin it into place around all

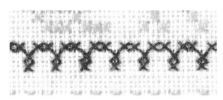

In her third border Mary reduced the amount of thread she was using, perhaps because she needed to conserve her supply of that color.

four sides on the front. Fold the ribbon over the edges and pin the back in the same way. Stitch down using the running stitch with #3371 floss.

Make a small bow with the ¼-inch ribbon. Run a length of #336 floss through the knot in back. Tack the knot in place to hide the seam where the two ends of the border ribbon meet. The original border design is disintegrating; all symbols ⊠ , ⊿ denote half-stitches in #3371. Half-stitches occur in other colors.

CHART KEY		
SYMBOL	DMC #	COLOR
✗	3371	darkest brown-black
O	3045	gold
U	316	mauve
◢	319	green
✳ ✱	336	navy 1 str., 2 str.
—	3832	cream: Au Ver a Soie®
●	2911	Au Ver a Soie®,
S	2912	Au Ver a Soie®,
⹀ ◨	924	teal blue: 1 str., over-1

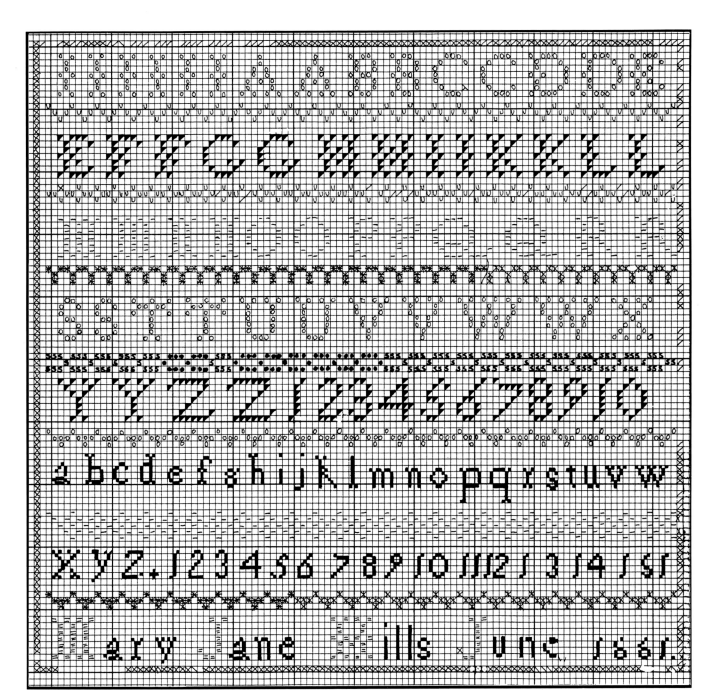

JULIAN CHAMBERLAIN

Nine-year-old Julian had ample time to work this, probably during an illness.

 It is rare to find a sampler done by a boy, since boys were not required to learn how to stitch, except as punishment or to occupy time when bedridden. A piece of work this extensive suggests the latter. An awkward stitcher like Julian would not have had the time or patience necessary for it if he had been sent to a dame school with the girls to learn stitchery in 1823.

Obviously, Julian was more interested in buildings than in flowers. The house on the left surrounded by trees probably represents his home. The other building, which looks barren and institutional, was probably his school. At the bottom he tried several new stitches. He must have liked the buttonhole stitch a great deal because he tried doing it in a circle—no easy feat, even for a girl.

Collection of Montgomery County Historical Society, Rockville, Maryland.

Julian appears to have been interested in architecture. Gazebos are rarely seen in antique samplers. In fact, the first ones were built only about 40 years before he was born.

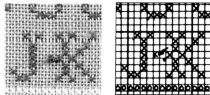

Julian should not have left waste knots or long, loose threads showing on top.

JULIAN CHAMBERLAIN
(16 x 11 ½ inches)

Considering that a boy's fingers worked the needle, and that he probably was not well at the time, this work deserves to be viewed with both sympathy and appreciation as a rare effort by a small boy born in a small Maryland town 170 years ago.

Julian tended to leave waste knots here and there on the front side of his work. (They are indicated on the pattern by the ● symbol.) If you want to replicate his original exactly, force yourself to leave waste knots at these points, unusual as that

may be. Though it is still customary to knot the thread on top and proceed stitching nearby, normally when the piece is finished, the waste

CHART KEY		
SYMBOL	**DMC #**	**COLOR**
+	729	gold, 1 str.
■	524	lightest green, 1 str.
X	501	blue-green, 1 str.
O	677	lt. yellow, 2 str.
V	370	olive green, 2 str.
⌂	503	lt. blue-green, 2 str.
T	830	dk. gold, 2 str.
S	924	teal blue, 1 str.
I	500	darkest blue-green, 2 str.
E	738	beige, 2 str.
•	842	tan, 2 str.
-	945/948	lt. pink: 1 str. ea., blended
H	3051	green, 1 str.
●	3047	lt. gold, 2 str.
▼	734	yellow green
⋌	926	slate blue, 2 str.
✳	3021	dk. brown: buttonhole & herringbone sts.

knots are cut and the loose threads woven into stitches on the back.

The General Instructions in the Appendix show how to find the starting point and work the stitches.

MATERIALS
22 x 17½ inches of 25-count mocha linen, dyed with #2 Coffee recipe (see Appendix); size 24 tapestry needle.

DIRECTIONS
Work this sampler with both one and two strands of floss. Refer to the Chart Key for the number of strands to use in each color.

Use the cross stitch throughout, except in the array of other decorative stitches beneath his name and the date, where it appears that he may have been experimenting. Instruc-

tions for working each of these stitches can be found in the Appendix: rococo stitch, satin stitch, herringbone stitch, and the buttonhole stitch. When you work the buttonhole, in #3021, note that the last stitch on the top right side is loose. The large **X** symbols in the chart at the bottom of the sampler refer only to #3021.

Shaded portions of chart indicate overlap with sections on facing pages.

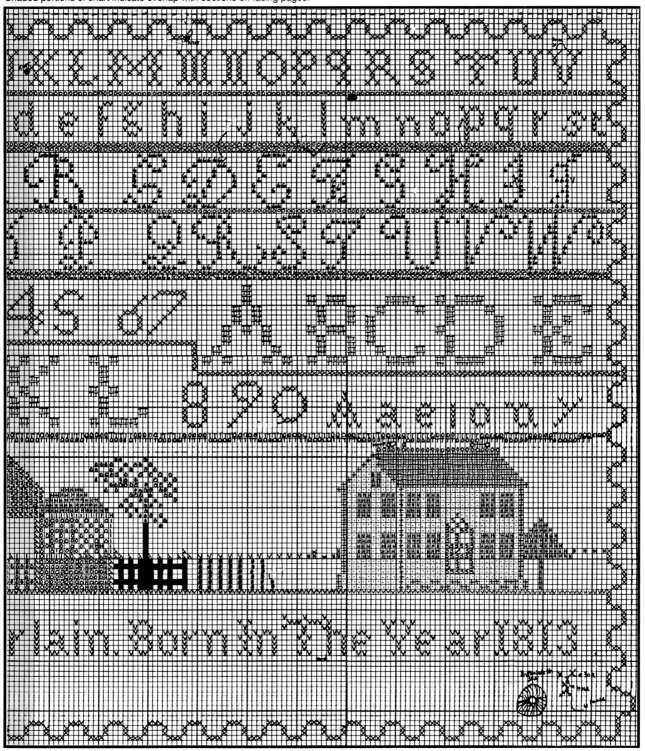

Drawstring Bag

Uniquely worked on 50-count linen and trimmed with a saucy red ribbon.

 This photograph shows an 1860s handbag in all its vibrant colors as it appears on display in the Smithsonian today. It was stitched on 50-count linen using rust, apricot, peach, blue, green, yellow, pink, light brown, and ivory thread—a remarkably contemporary palette for a sampler stitched over 125 years ago.

All that is known of the child who stitched it are the initials *E.G.* found on the bottom edge of both sides. She wrapped her verse around the bag and finished it with an hour glass. She placed her spirited array of decorative motifs—hearts, birds, trees, dogs (very rare), and eight-pointed stars—symmetrically on either side. At about eight inches square, it is the size of an evening bag or a young person's purse.

Collection of the Smithsonian Institution, Washington, D.C.

The thunder of that dismal word
Would so torment my ear
T'would tear my soul assunder Lord
With most tormenting fear

What to be banished from my life
And yet forbid to die
To linger in eternal pain
Yet death for ever fly

An hourglass commonly symbolized the inevitability of death as the sands of one's life slip away. The initials found near the bottom are the only remaining identification of the creative designer of this delightful accessory which, with a name in lieu of the verse, would look almost contemporary.

This gothic verse, which was worked entirely in over-ones on the front and continued onto the back of the original bag has been omitted from the chart because it is too difficult to stitch on 50-count linen.

DRAWSTRING BAG
(7 ⅞ x 8 ¼ inches)

The designer of this charming handbag put her initials, *E.G.*, along the bottom on both sides. Other than that, her identity is lost. The finished bag is 7⅞ inches wide by 8¼ deep and is made of a cotton fabric with 50 threads in the warp and 52 in the woof. She worked her fabric using the conventions of a cross stitch sampler, but arranged her design such that she must have intended at the outset to make it into a bag.

This work is rich in contrasts. The verse, and the hourglass placed at the end of the last stanza, both suggest the welcome approach of death. Yet she surrounded her verse on both sides of the bag with cheerful images of life—birds, hearts, trees, dogs, eight-pointed stars, flower baskets, and a saucy red silk ribbon.

The General Instructions in the Appendix show how to find the starting point and work the stitches.

DIRECTIONS
Work in cross stitch over one and two threads, in tent stitch, and satin stitch.

Many children immortalized favorite pets in their stitching.

MATERIALS
15 x 14 inches of 50-count tan cotton evenweave fabric; 2 yards of ½-inch, red ribbon (match #321); ½ yard red cotton for the lining (optional); DMC embroidery floss as shown in the Chart Key; size 26 tapestry needle.

C H A R T		K E Y
SYMBOL	DMC #	COLOR
S	301	rust
•	356	lt rust
L	734	lt. green
V	927	slate blue
+	367	green
T	3045	gold
■	776	pink
▬	435	lt. brown
O	822	off-white
E	738	tan
–	823	navy
k	632	brown

To construct the bag, enlarge this chart to 110% of the printed size on a photocopy machine and use the outline as a cutting pattern. Trace the pattern onto the linen twice, one pattern for each side of the bag. To make the symbols legible, enlarge the chart again to at least twice the printed size to use as your stitching chart. The symbols have been graphed at 20 squares to the inch. Stitch the motifs before cutting the linen. When you cut out the patterns, add ¼ inch all around as a seam allowance.

Place right sides together and stitch them together all around, leaving the mouth open. Turn right sides out. If you line it, make a bag of red muslin ¼ inch smaller than the pattern for the bag. Fit the lining into the bag and stitch the mouth of the lining all around the mouth of the bag. Finish the bag as shown in the photograph on page 151 by sewing a tunnel for the drawstring around the neck, binding the edge all around with red ribbon, and attaching small ribbon bows to the two bottom corners, front and back.

Fabric: All samplers are stitched on linen. The number of threads per inch woven into the linen vertically (the warp) and horizontally (the woof) varies. The correct thread count and the amount of linen to buy are given in the Materials section included in the instructions for each sampler. The instructions give the *design size* (the width and height your stitching will cover) in italics. The fabric size allows a three-inch margin on all sides of the piece. You need that much blank linen on all sides so the finished sampler can be framed properly.

Compare the 25-count linen on the left woven with 25 threads in each inch, with the 44-count linen on the right The extra space between every second vertical thread is visible in the more loosely woven linen.

It is important to purchase linen with the specified thread count if you want your finished piece to be the same size as the original. If you use linen with a different thread count —you may find a more open weave easier to see and count, for example—you can calculate a new design size by counting the number of stitches in the width and the height of the chart. Each square in the chart equals one stitch. Normally, one stitch is taken over two threads (though often over only one thread in parts of some samplers), so divide the number of squares in each dimension of the chart by the thread-count (number of threads to the inch) in the same dimension of the linen you buy. Divide the answer in *half* to get your new design size in inches because most of your stitches will be over *two* threads.

All machine-woven linen available today is evenweave; that is, the warp and the woof have the same number of threads per inch. Some of the antique samplers were stitched on handwoven linen in which the number of threads

per inch varies vertically and horizontally. The instructions for some samplers require that you make contemporary evenweave linen replicate the exact counts of the old unevenweave linen on which the original was stitched. The instructions specify the number of threads to remove from each inch of evenweave. Work down (sometimes across) the center of the linen. Slide your needle under each thread before you snip it so you will not cut the adjacent threads. Pull each half of the snipped thread almost to the edge of the linen on each side. Leave the last half inch of thread in the linen. Secure them there by backstitching each thread for a few stitches. Then trim the fringe and hand or machine-stitch along the edge depending on whether the edge will show when framed.

To prevent the edges of the linen from fraying, whipstitch them, as was done in the original antique samplers. (An easier method is to seal the edges with a glue such as Fray Check®, which can be dry-cleaned.) Pull long strands from scraps of linen to whipstitch or hem the piece unless the directions tell you otherwise. If you intend to hem your piece, work the sampler before you hem your finished work.

Hoops: Only one sampler in this book, that of Joann Isabella Gibbs, requires the use of a hoop, and that is used only to put in the tambour-work flowers at the bottom. When you stop work for the day, remove the hoop to avoid permanent stretch-marks. For all other work, hold the linen loose in your hands with a firm but relaxed grip to work the stitches. Do not leave your needle in the linen, because it will force the holes visibly to widen and, if it rusts even a little, it will discolor the linen.

Thread: Unless otherwise indicated, work all stitches with two strands of thread. The Chart Key and instructions indicate when to use one strand or more than two strands to replicate the varying thicknesses of the threads used in the original. The brands and colors of floss, or silk, (and, in one sampler,

wool) threads specified in the instructions for each sampler were chosen because they most closely match the colors of the original threads used in the antique sampler as it appears today, and because the color of a given number-code assigned by the manufacturer is likely to remain consistent from batch to batch. If the specified thread is not available, substitute the best color match from another manufacturer.

Starting Point: The original samplers were usually worked from the top down and the outer borders worked before the areas inside them. To locate your starting point, measure down three inches from the top and three inches in from from the left edge (or right edge if you prefer to start your work on the right side and work to the left). Start your first cross next to the nearest vertical thread as shown below.

Bring the needle's point up from the back of the fabric at X. Count up two threads, and over two threads to the right. Go down at O. As you work you will see that you are using the wider opening for each stitch.

Linen woven by machine today has a larger opening between the linen threads every second thread. (This regular variation is more visible in looser weaves such as 25 to 35-count.) If you make your first stitch next to the vertical thread with the larger opening it will be much easier to count your stitches. When you pull threads from evenweave linen to replicate unevenly-woven linen used in some samplers, counting the threads becomes more demanding because every stitch is not made at the wider opening.

Threading up: There are two ways to anchor the first stitch,: tying a waste knot (the method used by the children who stitched the original samplers in this collection), and the loop method, which is somewhat quicker, though less durable.

To create a waste knot, tie a simple half-knot (like the first knot you tie before you make the bow in your shoelaces) at the very end of the thread. Approximately one-half inch from the spot where you will make your first stitch pass the needle through from the front of the linen and draw the knot snugly on top. Then start working your stitches. When you run out of thread, snip off the waste knot, being careful not to snip the linen. (Some of the children did, notably George Eisenbray, as the mends that show in their work testi-

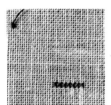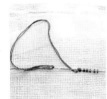

When the length of thread has been used up snip the waste knot. Rethread the needle with the tail on the back and secure it in the adjacent stitches.

fy.) Turn the linen over and thread your needle with the loose "tail" of thread hanging down where you snipped off the waste knot. Run the needle under the first three stitches on the back to bury the tail so the first stitch will not pull loose later. (Some of the children pulled the tails through to the front and left them hanging, as did Sophia Waters.)

You may use the loop method if you are working with two, or any other even number of strands of thread. Fold the length of thread in half and thread the eye of your needle with the two ends together leaving a loop at the other end. Come up from the back of the linen and do the first half cross. When you pass the needle through to the back, run it through the loop before coming up for the next half cross. Tug slightly to secure the thread in the loop.

Reading the Chart: Each stitch shown on the chart is marked by a symbol. The symbol changes to indicate a different color thread and, sometimes, a different number of strands of thread. The Chart Key in the instructions for each sampler is a legend for the symbols used in the chart. It gives the color number for the brand of thread used. Diagrams on pages 156 and 157 show how to form the stitches. The instructions for each sampler and sometimes its Chart Key explain which stitch to use in each area.

Over-Ones: When you follow the chart to work in cross stitch, you normally assume that one square on the graph represents one stitch taken over two threads in the linen. However, portions of many of the samplers in this collection are worked with smaller stitches called *over-ones*. To work over-ones, work the cross stitch in the normal way but cross each stitch over only one linen thread instead of the usual two threads. The chart will indicate two to four tiny individual crosses inside one square ▨ ▧ or will fill in the portion of the square to be stitched over one thread ◨ ◣. The Chart Key or instructions often tell you which parts of the sampler to work in over-ones.

Ending and Moving: When you have finished an area and wish to start stitching again in another area of the linen that is further away than the equivalent of three stitches (six linen threads), tie off your strands by running them through the backs of several stitches so no loose end shows. When the chart indicates that you should leave a loose thread, as the children often did in the originals, it is easiest to put them in later with small pieces of leftover threads. Secure them first to the back of another stitch with a knot and then pull them through so they cannot be pulled out accidentally. The children who stitched the original samplers in this collection often dragged their threads as far as they needed to before starting to work another area on the linen. If you copy them, the long tails could break if the sampler is laundered. Incidentally, it appears, when you see the originals, that many must have been worked with soiled hands and very few, if any, of the completed pieces were ever washed.

The linen used in antique samplers turns quite dark with age, a process which is accelerated with exposure to light. The instructions for each sampler in this collection specify which of the following dye recipes to use to approximate the color of the original.

Tea #1: In a kettle, boil enough water to half fill a large pan—a broiling pan, about 8½ by 13 inches works well. While the water is coming to a boil put five or six bags of ordinary breakfast tea into the pot. Pour in the boiling water and allow it to steep for about ten minutes. Wring out the tea bags into the water and discard them. Moisten the linen with plain water. Immerse it in the tea bath for ten minutes and check the color for a match, allowing for the fact that it will dry one shade lighter. Add one teaspoon of alum (which you can buy in a drugstore) and stir well before removing the fabric. Alum will set the color so it won't streak if you wash it later. Immerse the linen up to ten minutes longer if necessary for a proper color match. If you are uncertain, allow it to dry. Save the bath and re-immerse it if it needs to be darker to match the photo, but add new alum to the bath.

Tea #2: Prepare a large kettle of strong breakfast tea as you would for yourself. Bottle it when it cools and store it in the basement, or any dark place, for about three weeks. Follow instructions for *Tea #1*, above, substituting the bottled tea for the boiling water. It will be somewhat darker

Coffee #1: Prepare approximately six cups of breakfast coffee. Wet the linen in plain water if you want the dye to take evenly. (If you immerse dry linen in the dye bath it will color unevenly, as some old samplers have.) Immerse the linen in the coffee and proceed as described for *Tea #1*.

For **#2**, allow brewed coffee to stand for four weeks. For **#3** allow espresso coffee to stand for four weeks. For **#4** spray the finished, stitched sampler with Scotch Guard® to make the black #310 floss streak as the original has.

HOW TO WORK THE STITCHES

Photographs of the stitches listed in the instructions for the samplers in this book are shown, greatly enlarged, below and on the facing page. The numbers on the diagrams beside each group of stitches indicate the sequence in which the needle is brought up through the linen from the back and down again through the front. Bring the needle up at odd numbers and back down at even numbers. Though embroidery stitches have changed little, the names given to them often vary over and by location.

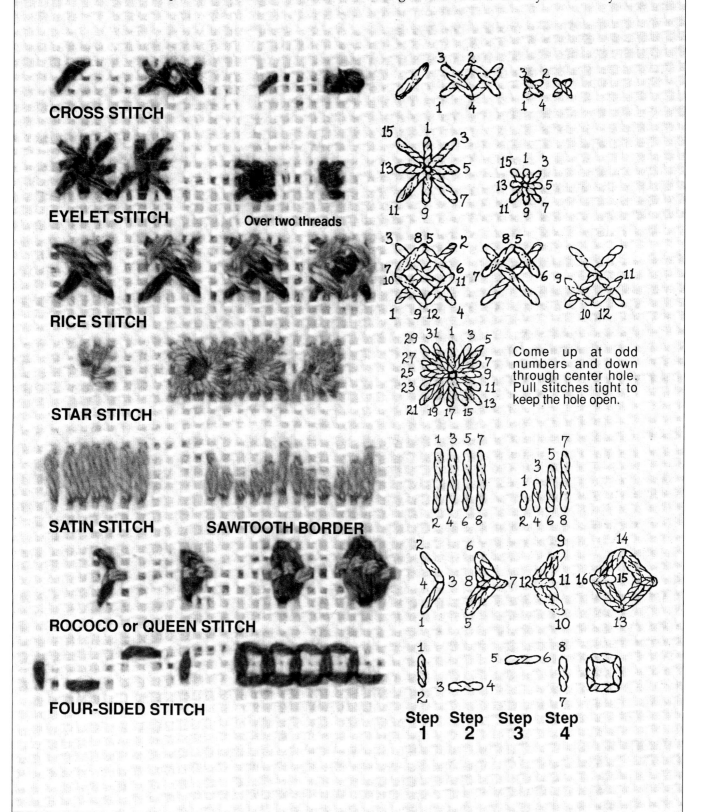

CROSS STITCH

EYELET STITCH Over two threads

RICE STITCH

Come up at odd numbers and down through center hole. Pull stitches tight to keep the hole open.

STAR STITCH

SATIN STITCH **SAWTOOTH BORDER**

ROCOCO or QUEEN STITCH

FOUR-SIDED STITCH

Step 1 Step 2 Step 3 Step 4

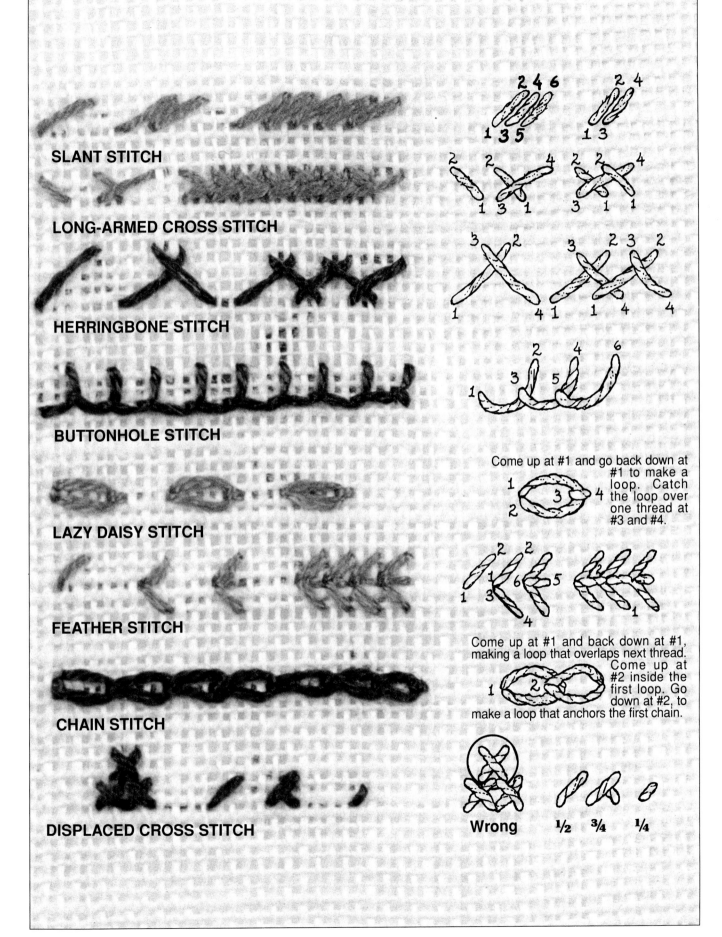

SLANT STITCH

LONG-ARMED CROSS STITCH

HERRINGBONE STITCH

BUTTONHOLE STITCH

LAZY DAISY STITCH

Come up at #1 and go back down at #1 to make a loop. Catch the loop over one thread at #3 and #4.

FEATHER STITCH

Come up at #1 and back down at #1, making a loop that overlaps next thread. Come up at #2 inside the first loop. Go down at #2, to make a loop that anchors the first chain.

CHAIN STITCH

DISPLACED CROSS STITCH

Wrong   ½   ¾   ¼

WORKING WITH A TAMBOUR HOOK

The Isabella Gibbs sampler on page 116 has tambour florals in the lower corners. After marking the design on the linen, place it in a hoop. To start, work one chain stitch with one strand of floss about 18 inches long. Let the thread hang beneath the linen and remove the needle. Insert the tambour hook one thread to the right of the hand-worked chain stitch (or to the left if you are working from right to left). Hook the hanging floss and pull it back through the linen. Count the holes in the linen between threads and re-insert the hook to start the next stitch, hooking the hanging thread and pulling it through again, and so on. (In the case of the Gibbs sampler, reinsert the hook at the next hole in the linen, because her stitches are very fine.) Secure the end of each strand of floss by running it through three or four stitches on the underside of the work. Since this is a chain stitch, a loose end can pull out all the work.

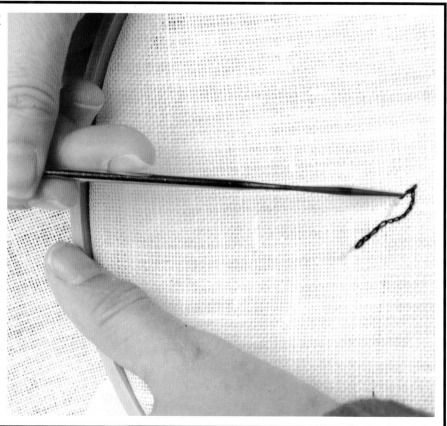

MARKING ALPHABETS

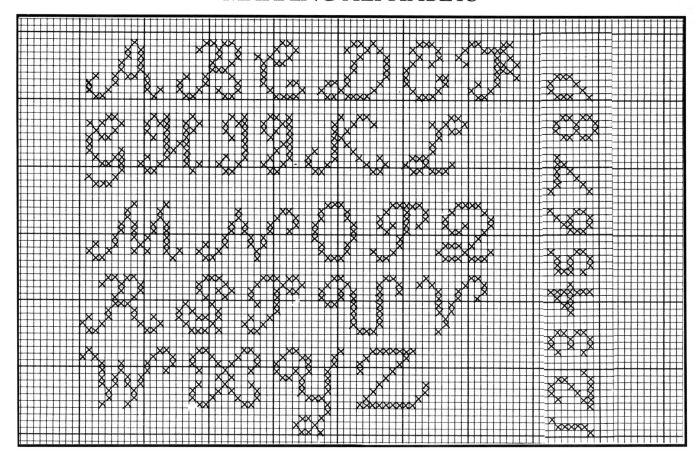

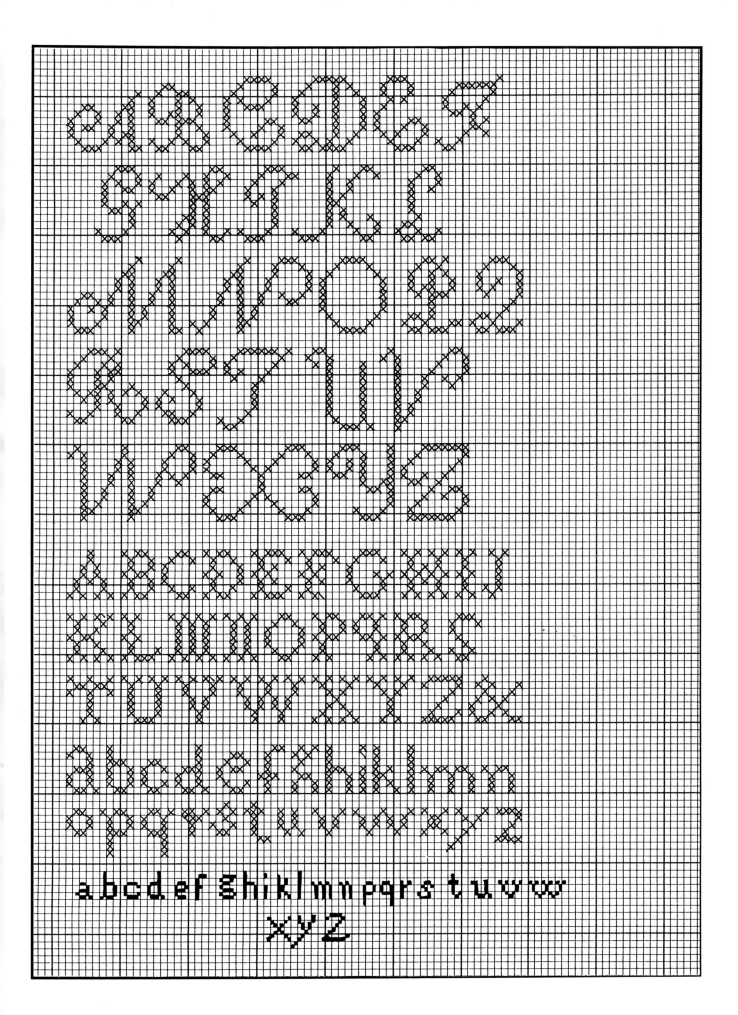

MOTTOES & VERSES FROM ANTIQUE SAMPLERS

Mottoes found on the earliest American samplers tend to be brief, stating the child's name, age, and the date the sampler was completed. The most common rhymes were "When this you see, remember me." (Lydia Tyler, page 36) and "[Mary Hill] is my name and with my nedle [needle] I did [wrought] the same." (Mary Hill, page 24). Like these simple epigrams, few verses stitched into samplers in the 18th and early 19th centuries were original. Most were copied from sermons, scripture, or other samplers and appear to have been lessons in humility as well as stitchery, e.g., the verses in the samplers of Mary Robinson (page 68), Maria Revere Curtis and Hannah Atkins (pages 76 and 100), and Elizabeth Kummer (page 122).

The following examples come from a variety of other sources, one of which is the most complete book on the subject—*American Samplers*, by Ethyl Bolton and Eva Coe, originally published in 1921 by the D.A.R. and since republished by Dover Publications, Inc., New York.

Caty Langdon is my name/And with my needle I rought the same/And if my skil had been better/I would have mended every letter. (1630)

Eunice Pettengil is my/name & with my ha/nds I wrought the/Same Steal Not Th/is For Fear OF/SHAME FOR Here You/Read The Owners/Name. I Wrought/This in The Year 17/91 Being In The 11T/H Year OF My Age/& WAS Born OCT 28/WN M [West Newton, Massachusetts] (1791)

Francis & Sarah Knowles My parents Dear/Paid for this which I have heare (1732)

Mary Ann Lucy Gries is my name/Marietta is my station Heaven/is my dwelling place and/Christ is my salvation when I/am dead and in my grave and/all my bones are rotten/when this you see Remember me/else I shall be forgotten. (1826)

In prosperity friends are plenty
In Adversity not one in twenty (1684)

Defer not til tomorrow to be wise/Tomorrow's sun to thee may never rise (1802)

A blind woman's soliloquy./Are not the sparrows daily fed by thee,/And wilt thou clothe the lillies and not me./Begone distrust! I shall have clothes and bread,/While lillies flourish, and the birds are fed. (Martha Perry c 1800)

In Mother's womb Thy fingers did me make,/And from the womb Thou didst me safely take;/From breast Thou hast me nurst my life throughout./I may say I never wanted ought. (1757)

Sarah Ann Souder worked this in great/ speed And left it here for you to read (c 1775)

Adam alone in Paradise did grieve,/And thought Eden a desert without Eve,/Until God pitying of his lonesome state/Crowned all his wishes with a loving mate./What reason then hath Man to slight or flout her,/That could not live in Paradise without her? (1796)

While hostile foes our coasts invade,/In all the pomp of war arrayed,/American be not dismayed,/Nor fear the Sword or Gun./While innocence is all our pride,/And virtue is our only Guide/Women would scorn to be defyd/if led by Washington. (1781)

When in Love I do commence/May it be with a man of sense/Brisk and arey [airy] may he be/Free from a spirit of jealousy. (1769)

Give me a House that never will decay/And Garments that never will wear away—/Give me a Friend that never will depart/Give me a Ruler that can rule my Heart (1792)

Beauty and Virtue when they do meet/With a good education make a lady complete. (1724)

When this you see, remember me/And bear me in your mind./What others say when I'm away/Speak of me as you find. (1785)

When two fond hearts as one unite,/The yoke is easy and the burden light. (1822)

No Star so bright/As my delight. (1792)

When I am dead and worms me eat/Here you shall see my name complete (1787)

This I did to let you see/What care my parents took of me. (1752)

Respect to parents always must be paid/or God is angered and they are disobeyed. (1784)

The Father fled to Worlds unknown/When aged fifty two/The Mothers left and may we all/Her virtuous steps pursue. (1805)

Now here you read that death has call my parents Dear,/and may we all for that day prepare. ((1816)

May I with innocence and peace/My tranquil moments spend/And when the toils of life shall cease/With calmness meet my end. (1810)

To Colleges and Schools ye Youths repair/Improve each precious Moment while you're there. (1786)

Delight in Learning Soon doth Bring/a Child to Learn the Hardist Thing. (1797

Though young in age And small in stature/Yet I have skill to form a letter. (1787)

My friends I hope you are pleased & so shall I/If this my work I may get credit by/ Much Labor & much time it hath me cost/I will take care that none of it be lost. (1767)

Please to survey this with a tender eye/Put on good nature and lay judgement by. (1815)